COMPUTING MADE S

GW00729184

AT ONLY £7.99 • 1

WINDOWS 95 MADE SIMPLE

WORD FOR WINDOWS 95 MADE SIMPLE
KEITH BRINDLEY

THE INTERNET FOR WINDOWS 3.1 MADE SIMPLE

ACCESS FOR WINDOWS 95 MADE SIMPLE
MOIRA STEPHEN

BESTSELLER
Works for Windows 3.1 (Version 3)
P. K. McBride
0 7506 2065 X   1994

Lotus 1-2-3 (2.4 DOS Version)
Ian Robertson
0 7506 2066 8   1994

WordPerfect (DOS 6.0)
Stephen Copestake
0 7506 2068 4   1994

BESTSELLER
MS DOS (Up To Version 6.22)
Ian Sinclair
0 7506 2069 2   1994

BESTSELLER
Excel For Windows 3.1 (Version 5)
Stephen Morris
0 7506 2070 6   1994

BESTSELLER
Word For Windows 3.1 (Version 6)
Keith Brindley
0 7506 2071 4   1994

BESTSELLER
Windows 3.1
P. K. McBride
0 7506 2072 2   1994

BESTSELLER
Windows 95
P. K. McBride
0 7506 2306 3   1995

Lotus 1-2-3 for Windows 3.1 (Version 5)
Stephen Morris
0 7506 2307 1   1995

BESTSELLER
Access For Windows 3.1 (Version 2)
Moira Stephen
0 7506 2309 8   1995

BESTSELLER
Internet for Windows 3.1
P. K. McBride
0 7506 2311 X   1995

Pageplus for Windows 3.1 (Version 3)
Ian Sinclair
0 7506 2312 8   1995

Hard Drives
Ian Sinclair
0 7506 2313 6   1995

BESTSELLER
Multimedia for Windows 3.1
Simon Collin
0 7506 2314 4   1995

Powerpoint for Windows 3.1 (Version 4.0)
Moira Stephen
0 7506 2420 5   1995

Office 95
P. K. McBride
0 7506 2625 9   1995

Word Pro for Windows 3.1 (Version 4.0)
Moira Stephen
0 7506 2626 7   1995

BESTSELLER
Word for Windows 95 (Version 7)
Keith Brindley
0 7506 2815 4   1996

BESTSELLER
Excel for Windows 95 (Version 7)
Stephen Morris
0 7506 2816 2   1996

Powerpoint for Windows 95 (Version 7)
Moira Stephen
0 7506 2817 0   1996

BESTSELLER
Access for Windows 95 (Version 7)
Moira Stephen
0 7506 2818 9   1996

BESTSELLER
Internet for Windows 95
P. K. McBride
0 7506 2835 9   1996

Internet Resources
P. K. McBride
0 7506 2836 7   1996

Microsoft Networking
P. K. McBride
0 7506 2837 5   1996

Designing Internet Home Pages
Lilian Hobbs
0 7506 2941 X   1996

BESTSELLER
Works for Windows 95 (Version 4.0)
P. K. McBride
0 7506 3396 4   1996

NEW
Windows NT (Version 4.0)
Lilian Hobbs
0 7506 3511 8   1997

NEW
Compuserve
Keith Brindley
0 7506 3512 6   1997

NEW
Microsoft Internet Explorer
Sam Kennington
0 7506 3513 4   1997

NEW
Netscape Navigator
Sam Kennington
0 7506 3514 2   1997

NEW
Searching The Internet
Sam Kennington
0 7506 3794 3   1997

NEW
The Internet for Windows 3.1 (Second Edition)
P. K. McBride
0 7506 3795 1   1997

NEW
The Internet for Windows 95 (Second Edition)
P. K. McBride
0 7506 3846 X   1997

NEW
Office 97 for Windows
P. K. McBride
0 7506 3798 6   1997

NEW
Powerpoint 97 For Windows
Moira Stephen
0 7506 3799 4   1997

NEW
Access 97 For Windows
Moira Stephen
0 7506 3800 1   1997

NEW
Word 97 For Windows
Keith Brindley
0 7506 3801 X   1997

NEW
Excel 97 For Windows
Stephen Morris
0 7506 3802 8   1997

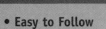

Works

for Windows 95
Made Simple

P.K.McBride

MADE SIMPLE
BOOKS

Made Simple
An imprint of Butterworth-Heinemann
Linacre House, Jordan Hill, Oxford OX2 8DP
A division of Reed Educational and Professional Publishing Ltd

ℛ   A member of the Reed Elsevier plc group

OXFORD   BOSTON   JOHANNESBURG
MELBOURNE   NEW DELHI   SINGAPORE

First published 1996
Reprinted 1997 (twice)

British Library Cataloguing in Publication Data
A catalogue record for this book is available from the British Library

ISBN 0 7506 3396 4

Typeset by P.K.McBride, Southampton

Archtype, Bash Casual, Cotswold and Gravity fonts from Advanced Graphics Ltd
Icons designed by Sarah Ward © 1994
Printed and bound in Great Britain by Scotprint, Musselburgh, Scotland

Contents

Preface

Works is an integrated suite, developed for the SoHo market. Let's try that again in English... Works is a set of programs, designed for the Small Office/Home Office users. The integration works at three levels.

- All use the same common set of core commands, so that when you have mastered one program, you are half way to mastery of the next.

- Any number of documents, from the same or different tools, can be in use at the same, so that you can flick quickly from one job to another.

- Data can be transferred freely between them, so that charts created from a spreadsheet can be copied into a report; lists of names and addresses, organised in the database can be merged with a standard letter to produce a customised mailing; word-processed memos can be taken into communications and zipped off down the phone line.

This book covers Works 4.0 for Windows 95, the latest version of this excellent suite. It has Task Wizards to simplify the creation of all manner of documents, and extensive on-screen Help. These, on top of an already user-friendly system, makes Works an ideal package for people who want to get things done – but don't want to have to spend too long learning how.

1 Starting work

Great works ...

Word Processor

Use this to write your letters, reports, newsletters and novels. The range of facilities on offer almost makes this a desktop publishing package. There are a wide range of typefaces, font styles and sizes, to be used for headings and for emphasis; headers, footers and page numbers can be added; text can be laid out in columns; and graphics, charts and tables can be placed in the text.

Spreadsheet

Use this to manage your cheque book, payroll, cash flow and all other aspects of your accounts – or anything else that involves numbers and calculations. With its DTP facilities, you can also use it for invoices and estimates.

Database

Use this to manage your stock, organize your address book or other sets of data. If any calculations are needed, this will produce a range of summary values, and data can be easily transferred between here and the spreadsheet.

Communications

With this, you can send and receive documents of all types over the phone lines (as long as you own a modem).

Take note

In Works, a Tool means one of these major or minor programs; a Document means a text or data file created by a Tool.

... and lesser works

- ❑ These can only be used from within one of the major tools.

ClipArt manages a gallery of graphics that can be placed in documents. Some are supplied with Works, and you can add your own graphics or bought-in Clip Art.

Draw is a graphics program with similar tools to those in Paint, though Draw works in a rather different way.

Graph lets you produce pie charts, line, bar and other graphs, from figures in a spread-sheet or database.

Note-It lets you add comments to text.. These are only shown when the reader clicks on a Note-it symbol.

Word-Art lets you create special effects, such as slanting or curved text, perhaps with shadows or other trimmings, for labels and headings.

Basic steps

❑ **To select a tool or a tab** on a dialog box, just click *once* on it.

❑ **To select an item** or file from a list:

either

Click once to highlight the item then click **OK** to confirm

or

Double-click on item to select it directly.

When you first come into Works, and whenever you set out to create a new document, you will meet the **Task Launcher** dialog box. There are three tabbed panels:

● **TaskWizards.** These create ready-formatted blank documents into which you can write your own text or data. The documents include letters – for many different purposes – invoices, address books, inventories, CVs, budgetting and more. If calculations are needed, the formulae are already there; all have text styles, colours and layouts ready set. And if the documents are not exactly what you want, they can be tailored to suit.(Page 4.)

● **Existing Document.** This takes you to a dialog box in which you can browse through your folders to select a file created in an earlier session. (Page 16)

● **Works Tools.** Use this tab to start a new word processor, spreadsheet or database document, or to set up a new communications link.

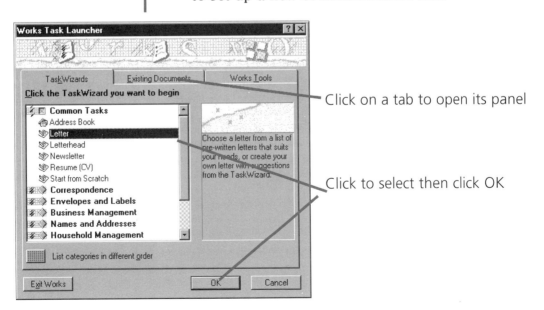

Click on a tab to open its panel

Click to select then click OK

Using TaskWizards

Any time that you want to produce a new document – of any type – check out the TaskWizards first. These cover 40 common tasks, and there may well be one that will produce a suitable document format for you.

The simpler Wizards need no further input once you have selected them from the list; others offer you choices of styles, or ask for information.

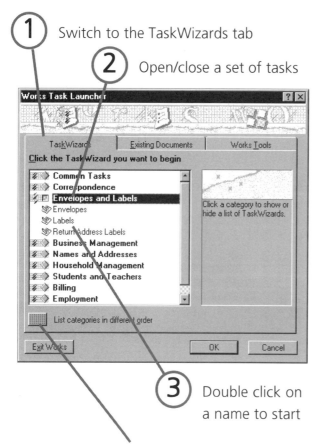

① Switch to the TaskWizards tab

② Open/close a set of tasks

③ Double click on a name to start

Wizards can be listed in different orders, but grouped by category is generally the most convenient.

Basic steps

1 In the **Task Launcher** dialog box, switch to the **TaskWizards** tab.

2 Click on a category heading to display (or hide) its set of wizards.

3 Double click on a Wizard to start it.

4 At the next panel, confirm that you want to **run the Wizard** – or select **show the list of documents** to open an existing document of the same type

5 Follow the prompts and make your selections as you work through the Wizard.

Tip

If you run a TaskWizard now – any one will do – it will give you a document to play with while you take your first look at the system.

④ Run the Wizard ...

... or list documents of that type

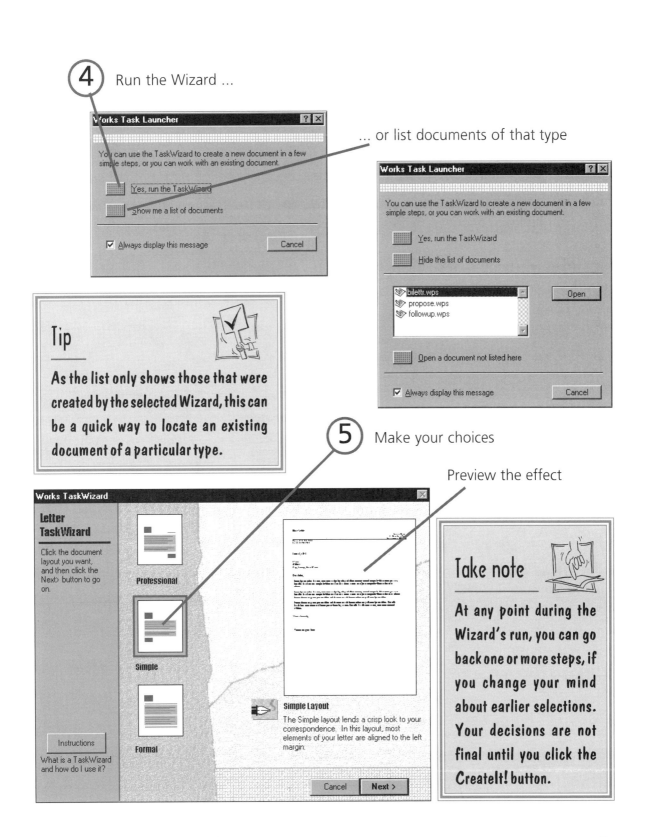

Works Task Launcher

You can use the TaskWizard to create a new document in a few simple steps, or you can work with an existing document.

Yes, run the TaskWizard

Show me a list of documents

☑ Always display this message   Cancel

Works Task Launcher

You can use the TaskWizard to create a new document in a few simple steps, or you can work with an existing document.

Yes, run the TaskWizard

Hide the list of documents

bilettr.wps
propose.wps
followup.wps   Open

Open a document not listed here

☑ Always display this message   Cancel

Tip

As the list only shows those that were created by the selected Wizard, this can be a quick way to locate an existing document of a particular type.

⑤ Make your choices

Preview the effect

Works TaskWizard

Letter TaskWizard

Click the document layout you want, and then click the Next> button to go on.

Professional

Simple

Formal

Instructions

What is a TaskWizard and how do I use it?

Simple Layout
The Simple layout lends a crisp look to your correspondence. In this layout, most elements of your letter are aligned to the left margin.

Cancel   Next >

Take note

At any point during the Wizard's run, you can go back one or more steps, if you change your mind about earlier selections. Your decisions are not final until you click the CreateIt! button.

The Letter TaskWizard is one that requires quite a bit of input the first time you run it. However, when you enter your address, phone numbers and other details for the **Letterhead**, they are stored and are reused next time you run the Wizard.

These lead to dialog boxes

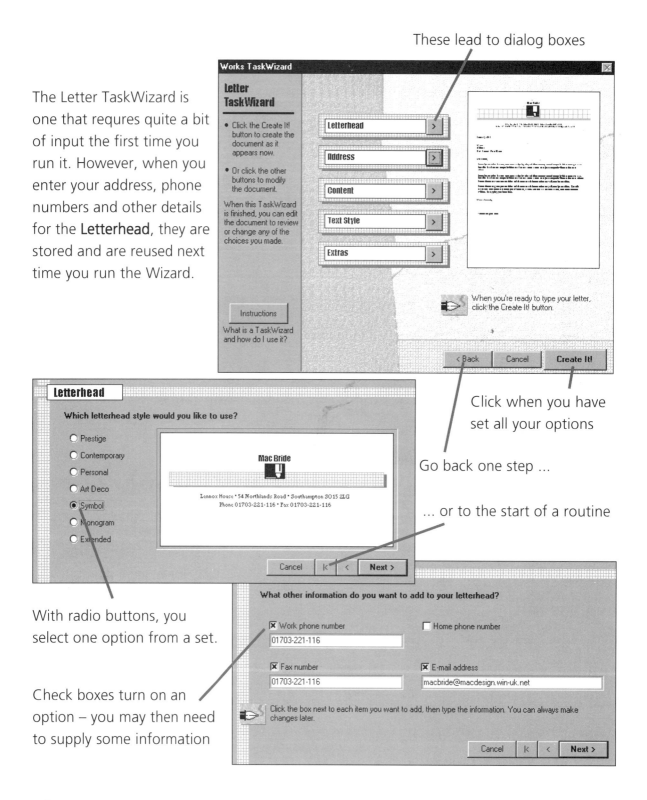

Click when you have set all your options

Go back one step ...

... or to the start of a routine

With radio buttons, you select one option from a set.

Check boxes turn on an option – you may then need to supply some information

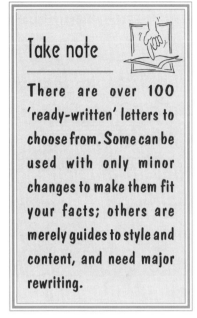

Take note

There are over 100 'ready-written' letters to choose from. Some can be used with only minor changes to make them fit your facts; others are merely guides to style and content, and need major rewriting.

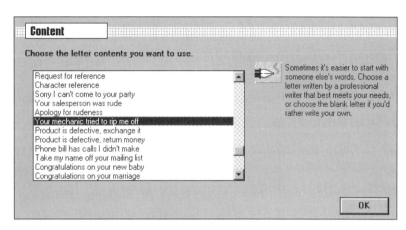

Many common situations are covered by sample letters in the Content dialog box.

Where you have made choices, you will be shown a Checklist before the document is created. If there are mistakes, you can go back into the Wizard to correct them.

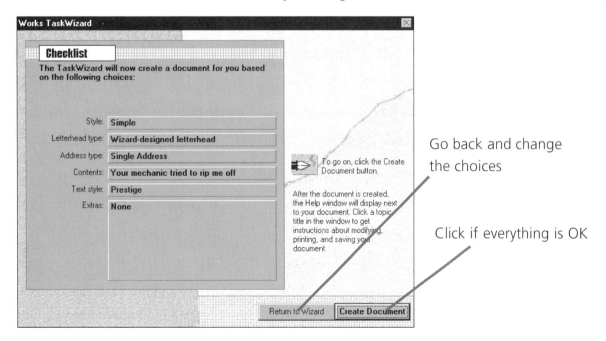

Go back and change the choices

Click if everything is OK

The desktop

Think of the Works screen as your desktop.

The main area – the **Workspace** – is where you lay out your documents. Each of these is in its own window, which can be minimised out of the way, or tucked beneath or to the side of the one you are currently working on.

Above the workspace is the **Toolbar**, containing buttons which can call up the most frequently used commands. Most aspects of font styles and settings, and alignment can be set from here. If a button is highlighted, it means that its setting is currently active. In the screenshot, the **Bold** button is the only active one. As a single click on one of these will replace two or three selections through menus, they are well worth using. You can add buttons to the Toolbar, or remove those you do not use. (See *Customising the Toolbar*, page 12.)

At the top of the screen is the **Menu Bar**, and the menus that can be pulled down from here, carry the full range of commands. The contents of the menu bar vary slightly from one tool to another. (See *The menu system*, page 10.)

At the bottom of the screen is the **Status Bar**. When you are selecting from menus or the toolbar buttons, this carries brief reminders of the purpose of the commands.

To the right of the screen is the **Help panel**. This can be shrunk out of the way to make more working space if you need it, or opened to give easy access to help. (See Section 2, *Getting Help*.)

Tip

Hold the pointer for a moment over the toolbar icons, and a *Tool Tip* will appear to tell you what the icon does.

8

Toolbar

Font name and size

Highlighted means active

Menu Bar

Tool Tip

Workspace

Help panel

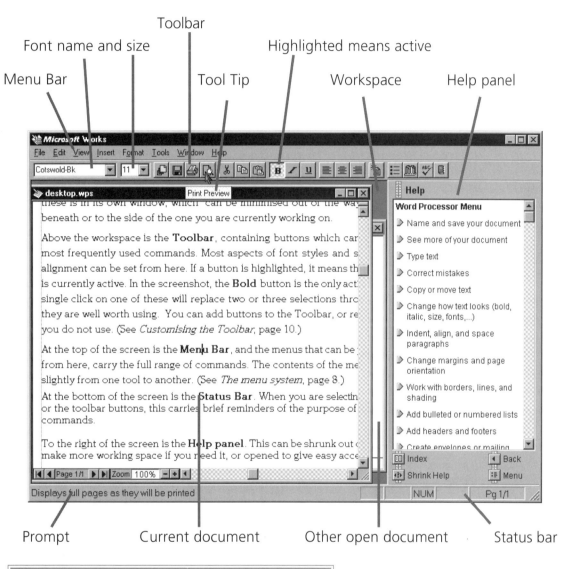

Prompt

Current document

Other open document

Status bar

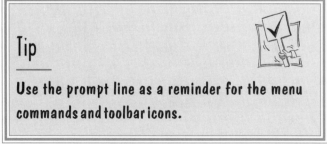

Tip

Use the prompt line as a reminder for the menu commands and toolbar icons.

The menu system

All of Works' facilities can be accessed through the menu system. The commands are grouped under more-or-less appropriate headings. The fit isn't quite perfect because not every command falls into a neat category. But finding a command is rarely a problem.

If you see a **tick** to the left of a menu option, it means that this is a toggle (on/off) switch, and that it is currently turned on.

If you see an ellipsis (...) after a menu option, selecting this will open a dialog box in which you will give further information or make detailed selections.

❑ **To select a command**

1 Point to a heading in the Menu bar and its menu will drop down.

2 If you do not see what you want, move the pointer along, opening other menus.

3 When you find the command you want, click to select it.

❑ **To abandon selection**

4 Click anywhere else on screen to close the menu.

① Click on a heading to open its menu

③ Click on the option

Toggle switch – this one is on

This calls up a dialog box

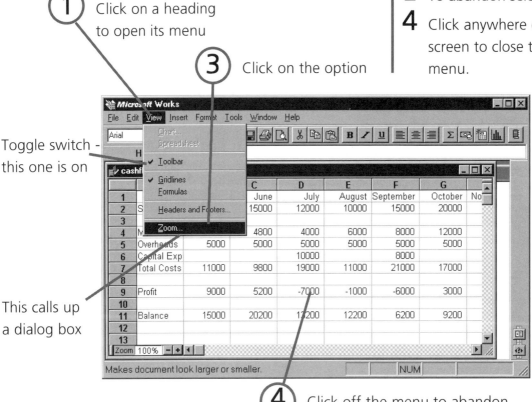

④ Click off the menu to abandon

Basic steps

To select a command

1 Press [Alt]. This tells the system to expect a key selection.

2 Press the underlined letter of the header to open the menu.

3 Press the underlined letter of the menu option.

To abandon selection

4 Press [Esc].

Selecting with keys

When you are typing in data, it is sometimes simpler to make your menu selections with the keys, rather than with the mouse. Some of the more commonly used commands have [Ctrl] key combination shortcuts, but all can be accessed via the [Alt] key.

The quickest method is to use the key letter of the menu choices, but if you want to browse, or use the [Left] and [Right] arrow keys to move along the menu bar and the [Up] and [Down] arrows to move the highlight to the option you want. Pressing [Enter] selects the highlighted option.

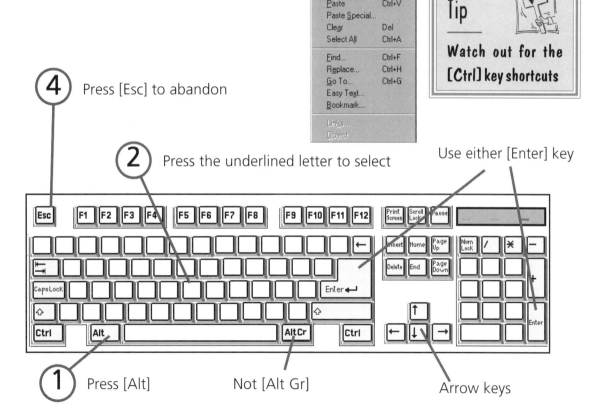

(4) Press [Esc] to abandon

(2) Press the underlined letter to select

Use either [Enter] key

(1) Press [Alt]   Not [Alt Gr]   Arrow keys

Customising the toolbar

Any time that you are working on a document, you can change the contents of the toolbar, adding or removing buttons. The changes that you make will be there whenever you use the same tool. So, if you add a Tab control button while working on a word processor document, it will be there for all word processor documents in future, though not for other Tools.

The **Customize Toolbar** dialog box also carries an option to **Remove Font Name and Point Size**. If you are not making regular use of these, clearing them away will leave more space for extra buttons.

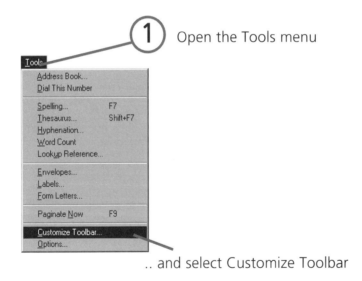

Open the Tools menu

.. and select Customize Toolbar

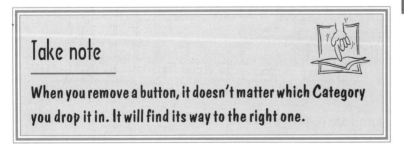

Take note

When you remove a button, it doesn't matter which Category you drop it in. It will find its way to the right one.

❏ **To add a button**

1 Open the **Tools** menu and select **Customize Toolbar...**

2 At the dialog box, select the **Category** (the menu heading).

3 Select the desired button and drag it onto the toolbar.

4 Release it wherever you want it to fit. The others will shuffle up to make room.

5 Click [OK] to confirm.

❏ **To remove a button**

1 Open the **Customize Toolbar** dialog box.

2 Select the unwanted button and drag it back into the box.

3 Click [OK] to confirm.

② Select a Category

③ Drag onto the Toolbar

⑤ Click OK

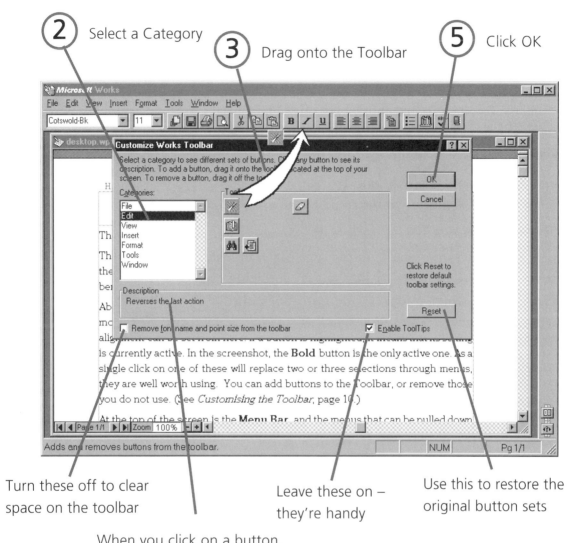

Turn these off to clear space on the toolbar

Leave these on – they're handy

Use this to restore the original button sets

When you click on a button, its description appears here

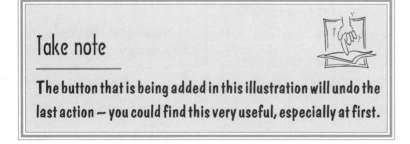

Take note

The button that is being added in this illustration will undo the last action – you could find this very useful, especially at first.

Saving files

While you are working on a document, its data is stored in the computer's memory. When you exit from Works, or switch of the machine, the memory is wiped. Sometimes, that can be a good thing. Do you really want to keep all those Thank You letters that you wrote after last Christmas? As long as you have sent printed copies off to your friends and relatives, you have no further use of them.

More often, perhaps, you will want to keep a copy of the document for reference, or to do some more work on in future. To do this, you must save it to disk.

The process is the same, whatever the type of document, and very simple. All you really have to do is decide on which disk and in which folder it will be stored, and what you will call it.

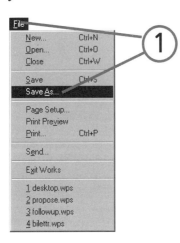

Open the File menu and select Save or Save As

Take note

If you have edited a document and want to keep a copy of the original, as well as the new version, use Save As and give it a different name.

❑ **To save a new file**

1 Open the **File** menu and select **Save**.

2 The first time you save a file, the **Save As** dialog box will appear to collect the details.

3 Select the **Drive** and the **Folder**.

4 Leave the **File Type** alone, unless you want to export the document for use with a different software package.

5 Type in a **File Name**.

6 Click ⬚ Save ⬚.

❑ **To resave a file**

1 Open the **File** menu and select **Save**.

2 That's it.

❑ **To save a file under a new name**

1 Open the **File** menu and select **Save** As.

2 Fill in the details as above, typing in a new name.

14

Extensions

❑ The **Works** extensions:

wps Word Processor

wdb Database

wksSpreadsheet

wcm Communications

❑ Other extensions that you may meet:

wmf Windows MetaFile (for Clip Art)

bmp BitMap from Paint-brush or other art programs

txt Text file from Notepad or another word processor

docMicrosoft Word document – Works can read those from Word (up to version 6.0)

Filenames

There are two parts to every filename – the **name** itself and a three-letter **extension**. The name is given by you to a file when you save it. Windows 95 sets no limits on the length or the characters you can use in filenames, but:

● the name must not be the same as an existing file in the same folder (or the new will overwrite the old).

● the name must *mean something to you*.

Don't bother about the extension. Leave it to Works to add a suitable one to identify the nature of the file.

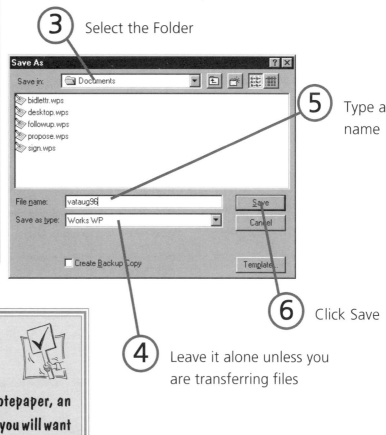

③ Select the Folder

⑤ Type a name

⑥ Click Save

④ Leave it alone unless you are transferring files

Tip

If you have created headed notepaper, an invoice or other document that you will want to reuse – with different text – in future, save it as a Template. (See page 18.)

Opening files

To get your documents back at the start of your next working session, you must open their files. Opening them is easy enough. The tricky part may well be *finding* them, especially as time goes by and your files start to run into their hundreds. However, Works goes a long way to make even this relatively painless.

❑ **From within Works**

1 Open the **File** menu and select **Open**.

2 Set the **Drive** and **Folder**, if necessary.

3 Pull down the **Type of files** list and select the type you want.

4 Select the file.

5 Click [Open].

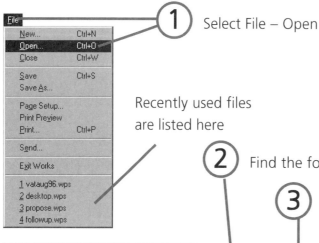

Select File – Open

Recently used files are listed here

(2) Find the folder

(3) Set the type

(4) Highlight the file

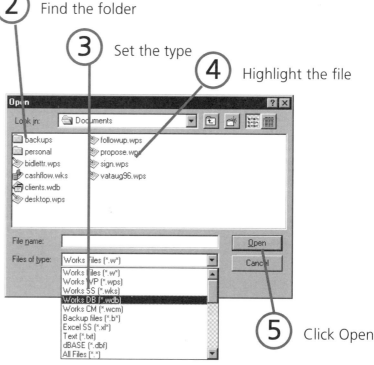

(5) Click Open

Tip

Works always starts to Look in the Documents folder. If you have relatively few files, keep them all in there.

If you need to several folders to organise your files, create them within Documents, where you can easily switch into them.

Basic steps

❑ **From Task Launcher**

1 Switch to the **Existing Documents** tab.

2 Select the file, if you can see it.

or

3 Click the **Open a document** button to go to the Open dialog box.

Tip

If you cannot remember where you stored a file, click on the "Help me find a document" button to go to the File Finder. (See page 20.)

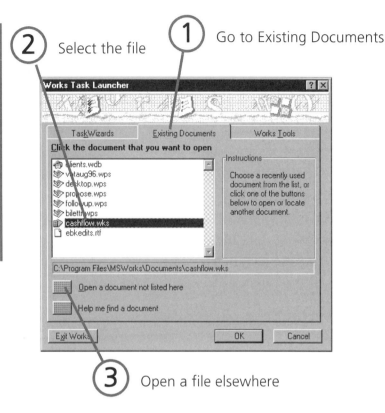

② Select the file   ① Go to Existing Documents

③ Open a file elsewhere

Transferring files?

❑ If you want to copy a file to or from another machine, running different software, check the alternative file types. There is probably one that will do the job.

Word processor documents can be saved and opened as plain Text or in Word, Wordperfect, WordStar and other formats.

Spreadsheets can be saved or opened as Text or in Excel or Lotus 1-2-3 formats.

Databases can be saved or opened as Text, Comma Separated Text or in dBase formats.

Templates

TaskWizards offer a quick and easy way to start new documents, but with templates, you have an approach that is even quicker and easier.

A template is a document that has all its formatting and permanent information in place, into which you will type new, specific text and data before printing. Headed notepaper is simple and obvious example of a template. Others include invoices, quotations, statements, certificates, invitations and thank you letters. With these and similar formatted 'blanks', the simplest approach is to use a Wizard to produce the first, save it as a template, then load in the template next time you want one.

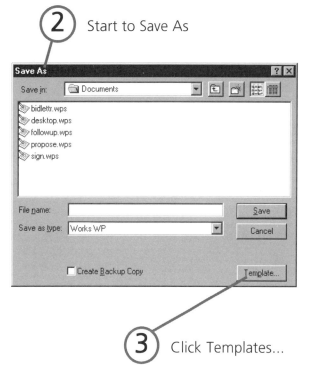

② Start to Save As

③ Click Templates...

Basic steps

❏ **Saving a template**

1 Create the document, with all its formatting and fixed text.

2 Start to save the file with **File – Save**, as shown on page 14.

3 At the Save As dialog box, click Template... .

4 On the Save As Template dialog box, type a name.

5 Click Defaults >> to open the lower half of the box to see – or reset – the current defaults.

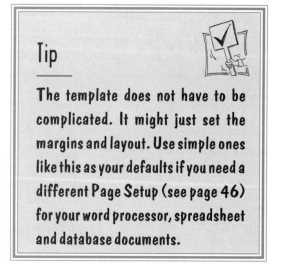

Tip

The template does not have to be complicated. It might just set the margins and layout. Use simple ones like this as your defaults if you need a different Page Setup (see page 46) for your word processor, spreadsheet and database documents.

6 If you want to make the template the default – so that it is used for all new documents (in that tool) – check the box.

7 Click ⬜ OK

❏ **Using a template**

8 Start to open a file as usual (page 16.)

9 Switch to the **Templates** folder and select one from there.

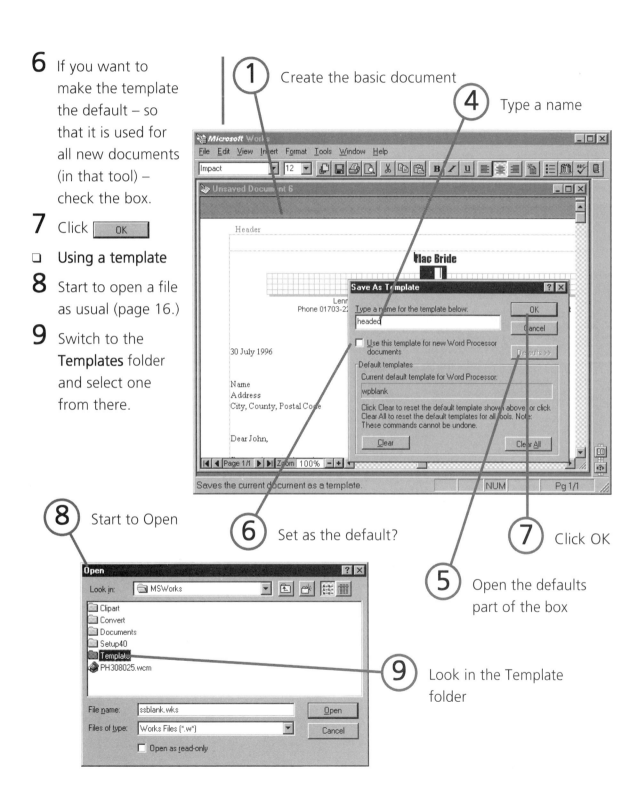

① Create the basic document

④ Type a name

⑧ Start to Open

⑥ Set as the default?

⑦ Click OK

⑤ Open the defaults part of the box

⑨ Look in the Template folder

File Finder

This is the same Find routine that you can call up from the Start menu in Windows 95. It can track down files by name, type, age, size or contents. As long as you have something to go on, no files need remain lost for long.

Give as much of the name as you can, using an asterisk if you want to leave a gap in the middle; e.g.:

'*DOC*' will find '*doc*ument1', 'Letter to *doc*tor', and any Word files with a .DOC extension;

'REP*.WPS' will find '*Rep*ort156.*wps*', '*Rep*lytoJim.*wps*' and similar files.

Basic steps

1 On the **Task Launcher** go to the **Existing Documents** tab and click the **Help me find a document** button.

2 Type in as much of the name as you can.

3 Tell it where to start to **Look** – it will search the **subfolders** unless you tell it not to.

❏ **To narrow the search**

4 If you know when you last worked on the file, open the **Date Modified** panel.

5 Set the **between** limits, or the previous months or days age.

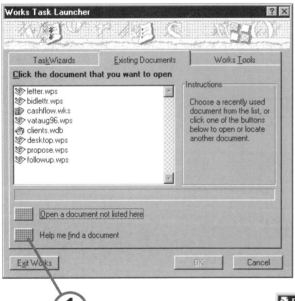

 Type as much as you know

Set the start point

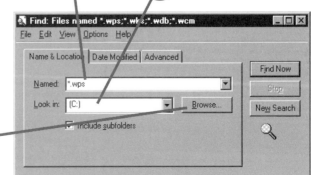

Click Browse if you need to find a folder

6 Open the **Advanced** panel.

7 Select the type of file and/or enter a phrase that you know is in the document – and not in others!

8 Click [Find Now] to start the search

9 Double click on a name in the found list to open the file.

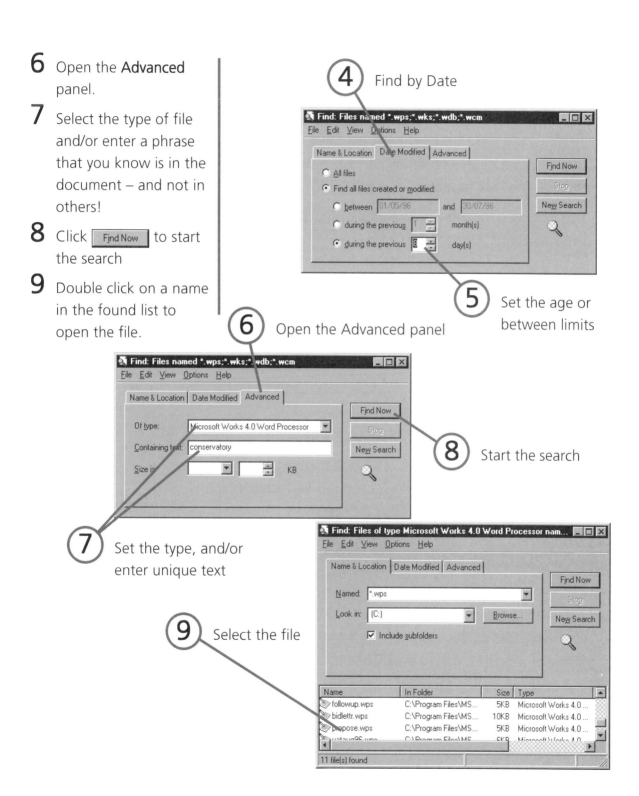

④ Find by Date

⑤ Set the age or between limits

⑥ Open the Advanced panel

⑧ Start the search

⑦ Set the type, and/or enter unique text

⑨ Select the file

Summary

❑ Works contains four main tools, **Word Processor**, **Spreadsheet**, **Database** and **Communications**, plus a set of smaller tools that can be called up from within the main ones.

❑ New documents are started and existing ones opened through the **Task Launcher**.

❑ **TaskWizards** offer a quick and simple way to create a wide variety of documents.

❑ You can open any number of documents from the same or different tools at the same time, though your workspace may get crowded.

❑ All of Works' commands can be reached through the **menus**. Point and click to select, or type **[Alt]** followed by the underlined letter in the menu option name.

❑ The **Tools – Customize Toolbar** command lets you add buttons to, or remove them from, your toolbar.

❑ Documents from all the tools are saved by the same **File – Save** command. If wanted, they can be saved in different formats for transfer to other software.

❑ Existing documents are recalled with **File – Open**. Works can read in files that were created by other leading applications.

❑ Formatted documents can be saved as **Templates**, and reopened later as the basis of new documents, with the basic structure and styles are already in place.

❑ The **Find** routine allows you to locate missing files through a combination of partial names, age, type, unique text and size.

2 Getting help

The Help panel

In Works, Help is always at hand. The Help panel is normally open all the time, for instant access. If you need the space more than the help, it can be shrunk out of the way, or completely hidden. In either case, it can be reopened easily at any point.

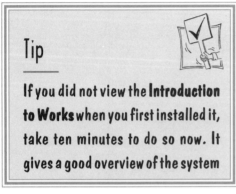

Tip

If you did not view the **Introduction to Works** when you first installed it, take ten minutes to do so now. It gives a good overview of the system

Basic steps

❑ **Making space**

1 Open the **Help** menu and select **Hide Help**.

or

2 Click 🔃 **Shrink Help**

❑ **Opening Help**

3 If the panel has been hidden, use **Show Help** from the **Help** menu.

or

4 Click 🔃 to unshrink.

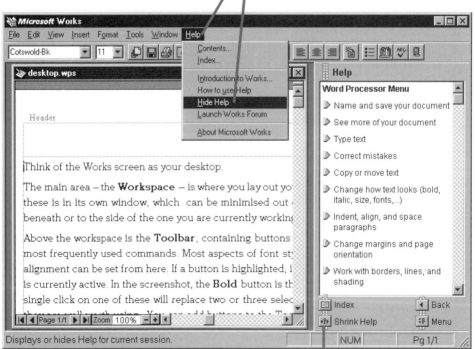

① Use Help – Hide Help

② Shrink (or reopen) the panel

Basic steps

1. Open the **Help** panel, if necessary
2. Click ⊞ **Menu**
3. Scroll through the topics
4. Click on one that meets your needs.

☐ You may then need to select through one or two levels of sub-topics.

5. Use the **Step-by-Step** guide while you work through a job.

or

6. Switch to the **More Info** tab for extra help.

Take note

If you run **Works** in a **Maximized window, the Help panel takes only 20% of the space — it looks larger here as the window has been reduced for the illustrations.**

Help from the panel

You can often find what you want by browsing through the Help panel. Just start from the top level of the menu and follow up the topic that interests you.

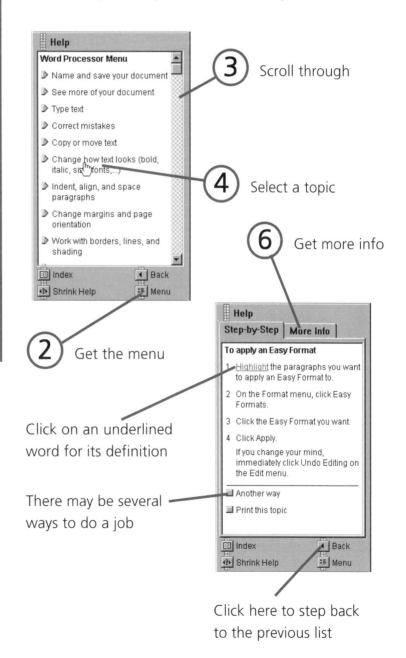

Scroll through

Select a topic

Get more info

Get the menu

Click on an underlined word for its definition

There may be several ways to do a job

Click here to step back to the previous list

The Help Index

Using the Index can be a quicker way to get to the right information, as long as you know what you are looking for. You don't have to be that exact, as the Help pages are cross-referenced. You can often get to the same page from several different start points, and once into the pages, you can easily switch between related topics.

The **Index** can be reached from the Help menu, or from Help panel.

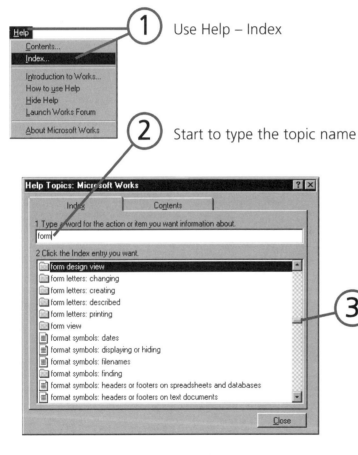

Use Help – Index

Start to type the topic name

Scroll through the list

If you can't see anything promising,
try a different key word for the topic

1 Open the **Help** menu and select **Index**, or click on the ▦ **Index** button on the Help panel.

2 Start to type a word that describes the topic you are interested in. As you type, the list of topics will adjust to show those that start with the same letters.

3 Scroll through the list until you can see a likely topic.

4 If necessary, open a folder to see its set of topics.

5 Select a topic to display it in the Help panel.

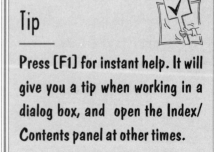

Tip

Press [F1] for instant help. It will give you a tip when working in a dialog box, and open the Index/Contents panel at other times.

To close a folder, just click on it.

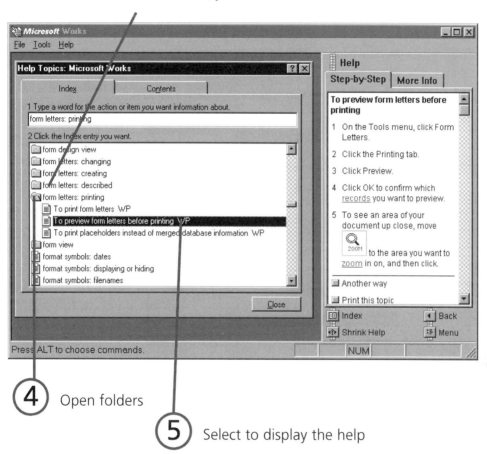

④ Open folders

⑤ Select to display the help

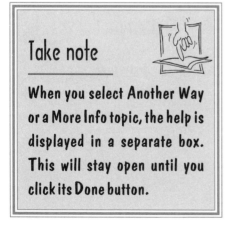

Take note

When you select Another Way or a More Info topic, the help is displayed in a separate box. This will stay open until you click its Done button.

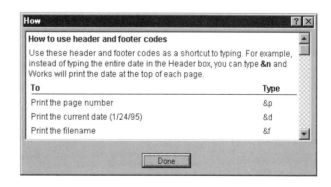

Help Contents

In the **Contents**, the Help pages have been organized into a hierarchy of topics. Start by selecting the tool, then work your way down through the levels of folders to focus on the help you need.

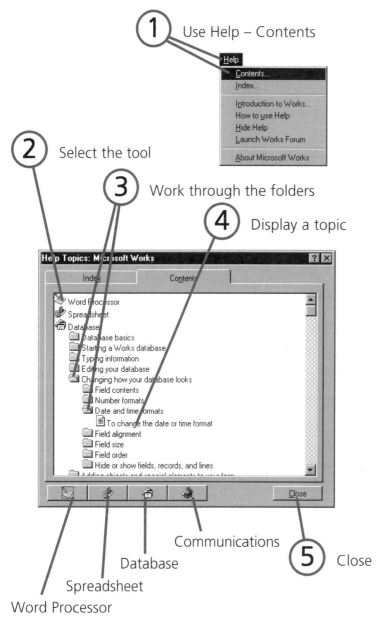

Use Help – Contents

Select the tool

Work through the folders

Display a topic

Communications

Database

Spreadsheet

Word Processor

Close

1 Open the **Help** menu and select **Contents**,

or

If you have been using the **Index**, switch to the **Contents** tab.

2 Click on a tool in the list or on its button, to open its folders.

3 Click on the folders to open (or reclose) them, until you find the topic you want.

4 Click on the topic to display it in the Help panel.

5 Click [Close] when you have done.

Take note

Contents gives you access to help on all the major tools, unlike the Help page Menu which only covers the current tool.

Basic steps

Other Help

❏ **Help in dialog boxes**

1 Click on the [?] icon at the top right. The icon changes to a query pointer.

2 Point and click on the item that you want to know about. A tip box opens.

3 Click anywhere off the tip box to close it.

When working in a dialog box, you can get help on any options within the box.

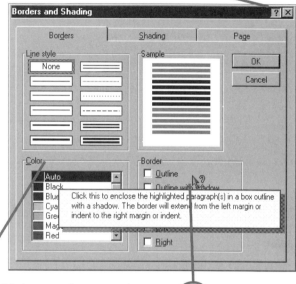

① Get the query pointer

③ Click anywhere to close

② Click on an item

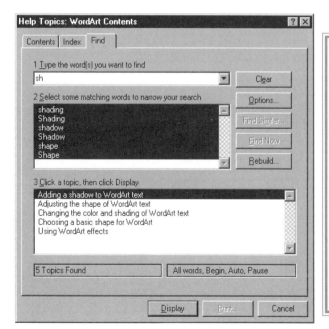

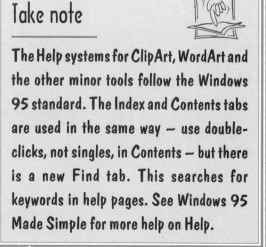

Take note

The Help systems for ClipArt, WordArt and the other minor tools follow the Windows 95 standard. The Index and Contents tabs are used in the same way – use double-clicks, not singles, in Contents – but there is a new Find tab. This searches for keywords in help pages. See Windows 95 Made Simple for more help on Help.

Summary

❑ Works offers plenty of help to its users.

❑ The **Help panel** can be shrunk or hidden if you need more working space.

❑ Click the Menu button in the Help panel to see the topics on the current tool.

❑ **Help – Index** will take you more directly you a Help page, as long as you can describe what you want.

❑ **Help – Contents** takes you to folders of topics. You will usually have to work through two or three levels of folders to reach a page.

❑ When you are in the Help system, you can go back over previous pages or move around related topics.

❑ Pressing **[F1]** will open the Index/Contents box or give you a tip on a dialog box.

❑ **Dialog boxes** carry a Query button to tell you more about the options in the box.

3 Working with text

Starting a new document

When you start a new document, there should be nothing in your main working area, apart from the faint outlines of the text and header (see page 56) areas.

The vertical, flashing, line is the **insertion point**. It marks the place where new text will be inserted when you type or paste it in.

The font name and size, alignment and margins shown on the toolbar and ruler will hold throughout the document – until you change them, though selected words and paragraphs within the document can have their own settings. If you want a significantly different appearance for your document, change the settings at the start.

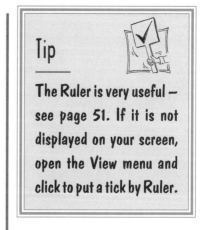

Tip

The Ruler is very useful – see page 51. If it is not displayed on your screen, open the View menu and click to put a tick by **Ruler**.

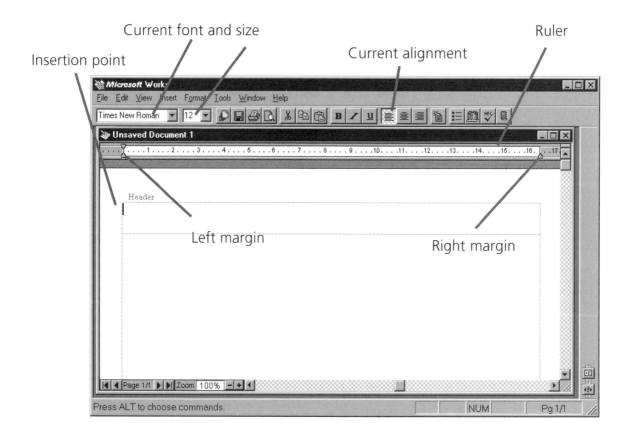

Insertion point

Current font and size

Current alignment

Ruler

Left margin

Right margin

Instant edits

❏ If you want to go back in the text, move the insertion point with the arrow keys or by pointing and clicking the mouse.

❏ If you spot any errors, **[Backspace]** erases to the left of the insertion point, **[Delete]** erases to the right.

❏ If you have missed something out, move the insertion point back and type in the words. Existing text will shuffle up to make room for it.

Entering text

Don't think of the screen as a blank sheet of paper. You cannot start typing anywhere you like. The insertion point can only move where there is text or spaces. If you want to start over on the right, type spaces or tabs to push the insertion point across. If you want to start lower down on, press **[Enter]** to move the end of document marker down.

A word processor is not like a typewriter. When you reach the end of the line, just keep typing and let *wordwrap* take the text on to the next line for you. Do not press **[Enter]** until you reach the end of a paragraph.

The advantage of wordwrap is that you can change the width between the margins, and the text will still flow smoothly from one line to the next.

[Enter] at the end
of paragraphs only

Keep on typing when
you reach here

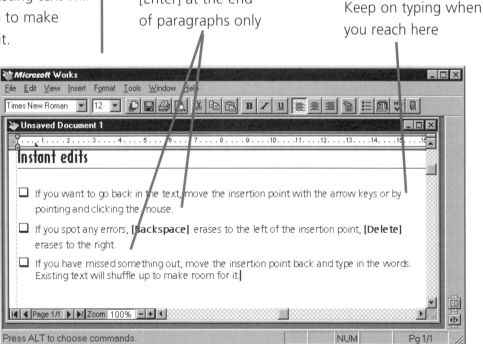

Selecting text

Basic steps

Text can be selected with the keys, but it is generally simplest to do it with the mouse. Once you have selected a block of text or a paragraph, you can:

● apply a font style or paragraph format – using the toolbar buttons or the Format menu. (See *Fonts and styles*, page 36 and *Indents and Alignment*, page 50.)

● delete it – press [**Backspace**] or [**Delete**]

● move it – see the Steps

● get it into the Clipboard – see opposite

❏ **To select a block**

1 Place the insertion point at the start.

2 Hold down the button and drag to the end.

❏ **To select a word**

1 Place the insertion point in the word and double-click.

❏ **To select a sentence**

1 Hold the [**Ctrl**] key.

2 Click anywhere within the sentence.

❏ **To select all the text**

1 Open the **Edit** menu and choose **Select All**.

Take note

A block of text can be any size from one character to a set of paragraphs or the whole document.

① Click at the start

② Drag to the end

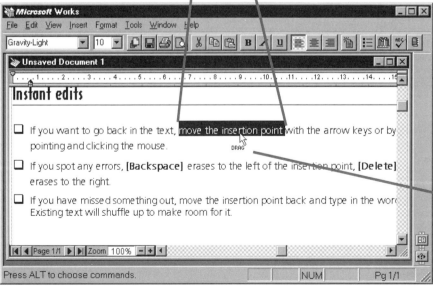

Instant edits

❏ If you want to go back in the text, move the insertion point with the arrow keys or by pointing and clicking the mouse.

❏ If you spot any errors, [**Backspace**] erases to the left of the insertion point, [**Delete**] erases to the right.

❏ If you have missed something out, move the insertion point back and type in the word. Existing text will shuffle up to make room for it.

DRAG turns to MOVE or COPY as you drag it

Basic steps

Using the Clipboard

❑ **To drag and drop selected text**

1 Point anywhere within the selected block.

2 Hold down the left button and drag the insertion point. You will see MOVE beside the pointer.

3 Release the button to drop the text in at the insertion point.

❑ **To copy selected text**

1 Point anywhere within the block.

2 Hold down [Ctrl] while you drag. You will see COPY by the pointer.

3 Release the button to drop in the text.

Dragging and dropping text can only be done within a document – and can only be done easily when you are not moving the block very far. To move a block over a distance, or from one document to another, you must use the **Edit** menu or toolbar buttons. Text can be cut or copied from your document into the Clipboard, and pasted wherever you want it. Learn the [Ctrl] keystrokes for these commands – they are the same in all Windows applications.

● **Edit – Cut** [Ctrl]–[X] removes the original text, storing a copy in the Clipboard;

● **Edit – Copy** [Ctrl]–[C] copies the text into the Clipboard;

● **Edit – Paste** [Ctrl]–[V] inserts a copy of whatever is in the Clipboard.

These are on the Edit menu of all Windows applications

This will select the whole text

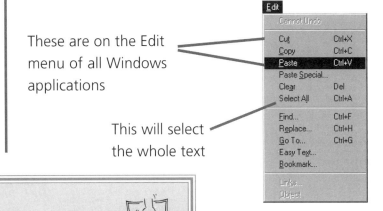

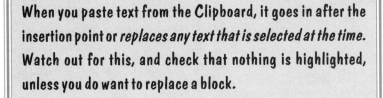

Take note

When you paste text from the Clipboard, it goes in after the insertion point or *replaces any text that is selected at the time.* Watch out for this, and check that nothing is highlighted, unless you do want to replace a block.

Fonts and styles

Font styles can be applied in two different ways.

● You can set them at the start, or at any point, to apply to everything you type afterwards – until you change them again.

● You can select a block, **anywhere in the middle of the text,** and apply a format to that block only.

All aspects of the appearance of text can be set through the **Format** menu, but if you are changing one feature only, it is often quicker to use the toolbar buttons or the keyboard shortcuts.

Basic steps

1 If you are formatting a block, select it first.

2 Open the **Format** menu and select **Font and Style...**

3 At the dialog box, start by selecting a **Font** from the list.

4 Change the **Size, Style** and other aspects next, checking the appearance of the text in the **Sample** pane.

5 Click [OK] when you are done.

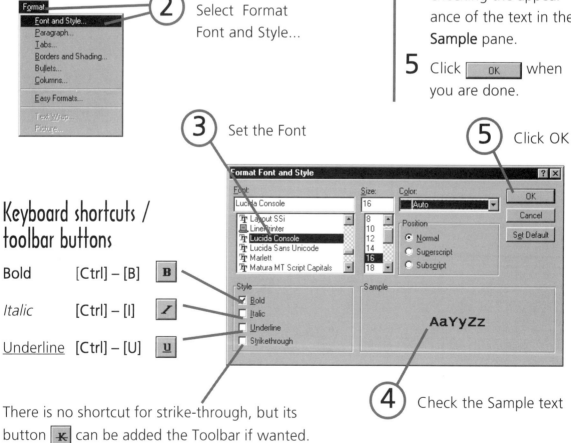

Select Format Font and Style...

Set the Font

Click OK

Check the Sample text

Keyboard shortcuts / toolbar buttons

Bold   [Ctrl] – [B]   **B**

Italic   [Ctrl] – [I]   *I*

Underline [Ctrl] – [U]   U

There is no shortcut for strike-through, but its button 𝐤 can be added the Toolbar if wanted.

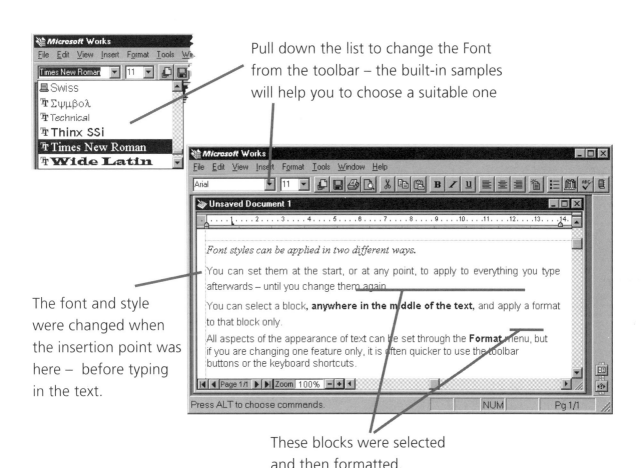

Pull down the list to change the Font from the toolbar – the built-in samples will help you to choose a suitable one

The font and style were changed when the insertion point was here – before typing in the text.

These blocks were selected and then formatted.

Text sizes

9 point or less is for footnotes

12 point gives clear readable text

14 point works for sub-headings

18 point is good for titles

36 point makes a headline

Find and Replace

A simple **Find** will locate the next occurrence of a given word or phrase. You can use it to check documents for references to particular items, when you do not know if they are there or not. You can also use it to jump to a part of the document identified by a key word. The longer the document, the more useful this becomes.

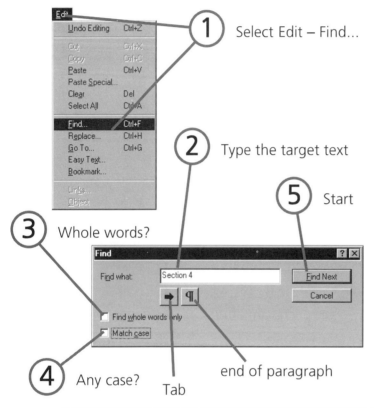

Select Edit – Find...

Type the target text

Start

Whole words?

Any case?   Tab   end of paragraph

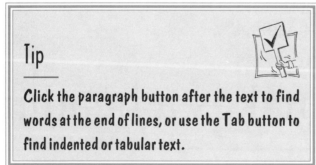

Tip

Click the paragraph button after the text to find words at the end of lines, or use the Tab button to find indented or tabular text.

1 Open the **Edit** menu and select **Find**.

2 Type in the word or phrase you want to find.

3 If it might form part of a longer word, then check the **Match Whole Word Only** option.

4 If the pattern of capitals and lower case is important, check the **Match Case** option.

5 Click `Find Next` to start the search.

6 If the text is present, it will be found and highlighted. You can then either look for the next occurrence, or **Cancel** to return to the document – at the site of the found text.

Basic steps

1 Open the **Edit** menu and select **Replace**.

2 Type in the word or phrase you want to find, and the text that is to replace it.

3 Check the **Match Whole Word Only** and **Match Case** options if appropriate.

4 If you only want re-place some of the occurrences, click
[**Find Next**] to start, then click [Replace] when appropriate.

5 If you want a clean sweep, click [Replace All]

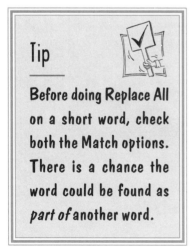

Tip

Before doing Replace All on a short word, check both the Match options. There is a chance the word could be found as *part of* another word.

Find and Replace will find the given text and replace it with a new phrase. it is said that some unscrupulous authors use this to make new books from old. A quick Replace on the names of the key characters and of the places, and you have a fresh novel!

It is more commonly used as a time-saver. If you had a long name, such as "Butterworth-Heinemann", that had to be written several times in a document, you could type an abbreviation, "B-H", and later use Replace to swap the full name back in.

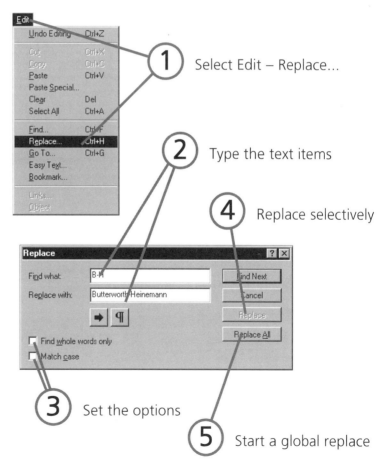

(1) Select Edit – Replace...

(2) Type the text items

(4) Replace selectively

(3) Set the options

(5) Start a global replace

39

Easy text

Do you find that there are some phrases or sentences that you use often – standard openings or closures to letters, client's addresses, long product names, or whatever? Easy Text can handle these. Just type the text once, and in future you will be able to call it up with a couple of mouse clicks.

1 Open the **Insert** menu, point to **Easy Text** and select **New Easy Text...**

2 Enter a name in the top slot

3 Type your text in the box below.

4 Click Done

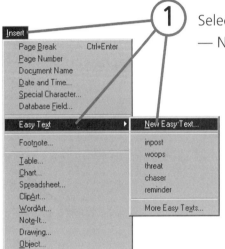

Select Insert — Easy Text — New Easy Text

2 Give it a name

3 Type the text

4 Click Done

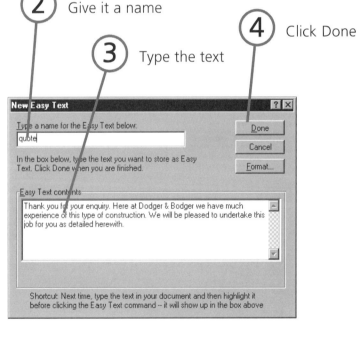

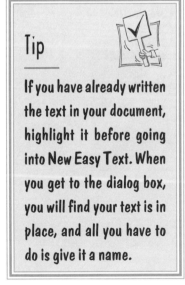

Tip

If you have already written the text in your document, highlight it before going into New Easy Text. When you get to the dialog box, you will find your text is in place, and all you have to do is give it a name.

40

Basic steps

❑ **To insert Easy Text**

1 Position your insertion point where you want the text to go.

2 Open the **Insert** menu, point to **Easy Text** and pick the text or select **More Easy Text...**

or

2 Open the **Edit** menu and select **Easy Text...**

3 Pick the text you want from the list.

4 Click ☐ Insert

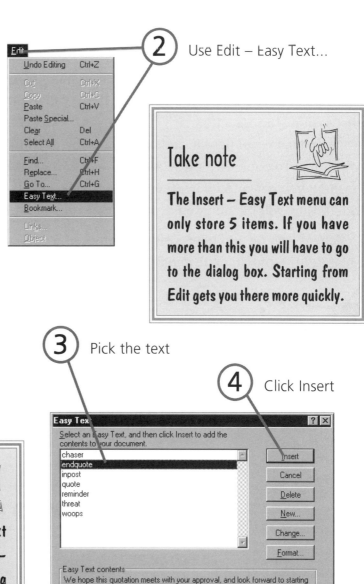

② Use Edit – Easy Text...

③ Pick the text

④ Click Insert

Take note

The Insert – Easy Text menu can only store 5 items. If you have more than this you will have to go to the dialog box. Starting from Edit gets you there more quickly.

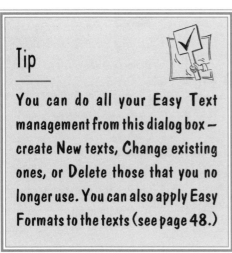

Tip

You can do all your Easy Text management from this dialog box – create **New** texts, **Change** existing ones, or **Delete** those that you no longer use. You can also apply Easy Formats to the texts (see page 48.)

Spelling

Even the best spellers need these! You may not make spelling mistakes, but is your typing perfect?

The spelling checker works from a dictionary of over 100,000 words. It's a good number, but there will be some words that you use that are not present. Specialised terms and names of people and places are the most likely omissions. To cope with these, there is a user dictionary, to which you can add your own selection of words. Once added, they will be included in spelling checks in future.

The check can be run over a single, selected word, over a highlighted block, or throughout the document.

Select Tools – Spelling

Change? Ignore?

Useful for skipping filenames,
references and technical stuff

1 If you only want to check one word, or a block, select it first.

2 Open the **Tools** menu and select **Spelling...** or click

3 When an unknown word is found, it is highlighted and the dialog box opens with these options:

> Change   replace with the word in the Change To slot – you can edit this first if you want

> Change All   replace with this word every time

> Ignore   It's OK, leave it...

> Ignore All   ... every time you see it

> Add   Add to your personal dictionary

> Suggest   Brings up a list of possibilities – likely ones are suggested automatically

Basic steps

1 Select the word you would like to replace.

2 Open the **Tools** menu and select **Thesaurus** or click if you have added it to your toolbar.

3 If the word can have several **Meanings**, select the closest from the list on the left.

4 Select a word from the **Synonyms** list on the right.

5 Click [Replace] to replace the word with the current synonym.

Thesaurus

Stuck for *le mot juste*? Let the Thesaurus suggest (offer, propound, submit, advise, propose) a better (preferred, improved, superior) word. With a bank of just under 200,000 words to draw from, it can generally come up with something suitable (apropos, pertinent, relevant, applicable, germane).

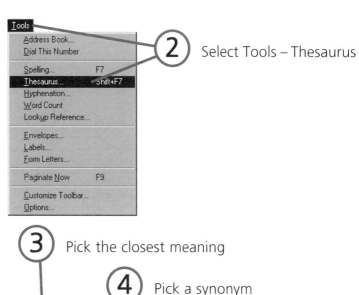

② Select Tools – Thesaurus

③ Pick the closest meaning

④ Pick a synonym

⑤ Click Replace

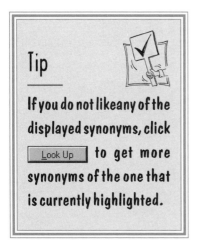

Tip

If you do not like any of the displayed synonyms, click [Look Up] to get more synonyms of the one that is currently highlighted.

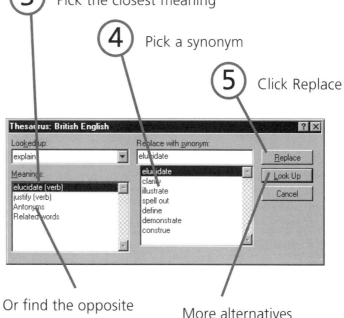

Or find the opposite

More alternatives

43

Summary

❏ When you start a new document, there are default settings for fonts and formats already in place. Change these at the start if you want a different appearance.

❏ The **Insertion Point** shows where text will appear when you type. Move it with the arrow keys or the mouse if you want to go back into your text to edit it.

❏ Corrections can be made as you type by pressing **[Backspace]**, or left for tidying up later.

❏ A **selected** block of text can be formatted, deleted or moved to a new position.

❏ The Clipboard's **Edit Cut** and **Paste** facilities allow you to copy and move text between pages and between documents.

❏ **Find** will search documents for particular words, and can be used to jump to the location of a word.

❏ **Replace** lets you type in abbreviations, and replace them all at the end in a single operation.

❏ Use **Easy Text** to save retyping those phrases and sentences that you use often.

❏ The **Spelling** checker is an invaluable aid for spotting mistypes, as well as spelling errors.

❏ The **Thesaurus** can help you to find the most appropriate words to express your meaning.

4 Working on layout

Page setup

Before you get too far into typing the text, you should check that the basic layout of the page is right. Use the **Page Setup** routine to set the paper size, orientation and margins. And check the effect of these settings with **Print Preview** or by switching to **Page Layout** view.

1 From the **File** menu select **Page Setup...**

2 Set the **Margins** to suit.

3 Open the **Source, Size & Orientation** panel. Check the **Paper size**. Change the **Orientation** to *Landscape* if you want to print sideways.

4 Leave **Other Options** for now. Click [OK]

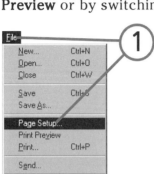

Select File – Page Setup...

The Sample gives a rough idea of how a page will look.

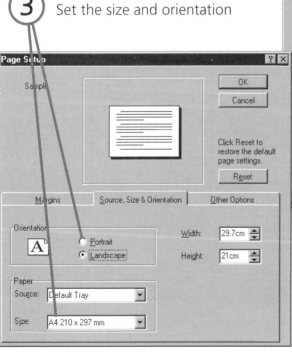

Set the size and orientation

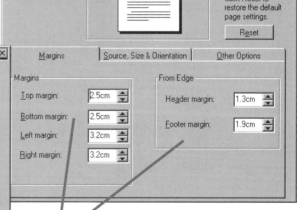

Set the Margins – Header and Footer margins must be less than Top and Bottom margins

Basic steps

1 Open the **File** menu and select **Print Preview..** or click on the ▣ button.

2 If you want to take a closer look, don't use the button. Point the magnifying glass and click – it gets you to the right place. Click again to get even closer, and a third time to switch back to the full page.

3 Click [Cancel] to return to editing.

See also *Printing*, page 60.

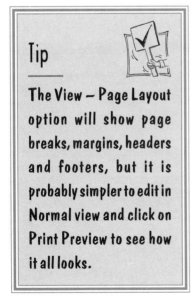

Tip

The View – Page Layout option will show page breaks, margins, headers and footers, but it is probably simpler to edit in Normal view and click on Print Preview to see how it all looks.

Print Preview

Works is a WYSIWYG (What You See Is What You Get) system, but there are usually subtle difference between the screen and the printed version. Use Print Preview whenever you are making adjustments to the layout or the fonts.

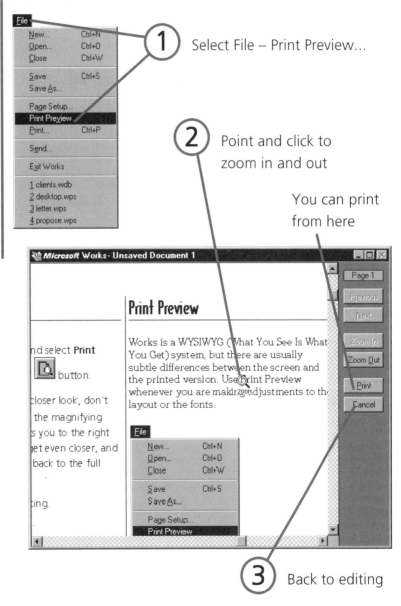

① Select File – Print Preview...

② Point and click to zoom in and out

You can print from here

③ Back to editing

Easy Formats

These offer a quick and simple approach to formatting paragraphs. With a couple of clicks you can apply a complete format – font type, size and style, layout, borders and shades.

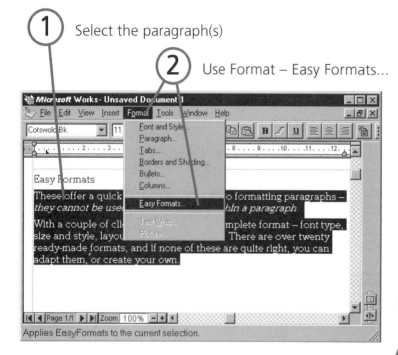

(1) Select the paragraph(s)

(2) Use Format – Easy Formats...

1 Select the paragraphs you want to format, or place the insertion point where you want to type new text, using the chosen format.

2 From the **Format** menu select **Easy Formats...**

3 Work through the list, clicking on formats to see the sample.

4 When you find one you like, click [Apply]

(3) Sample the formats

(4) Apply a format

Take note

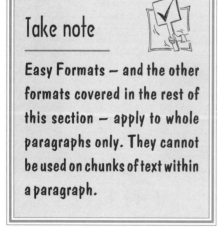

Easy Formats – and the other formats covered in the rest of this section – apply to whole paragraphs only. They cannot be used on chunks of text within a paragraph.

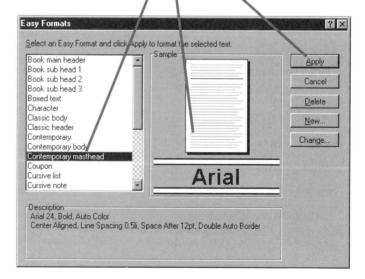

Basic steps

1 Start from the Easy Formats... dialog

2 Click `Change...` to adjust an existing format or `New...` to create one from scratch. Both get you to the same place.

3 Type in a name if creating a new format.

4 Click the button for the aspect of the format you want to define.

5 Click `Done`

Take note

You can use Easy Formats to set up a 'house style'. This will give the same look and feel to all your letters, reports, memos or newsletters.

New Easy Formats

There are over twenty ready-made formats, but if none of these are quite right for your purposes, you can adapt them, or create new ones.

Tip

When changing an existing format, give it a new name if you want to retain the original for later use.

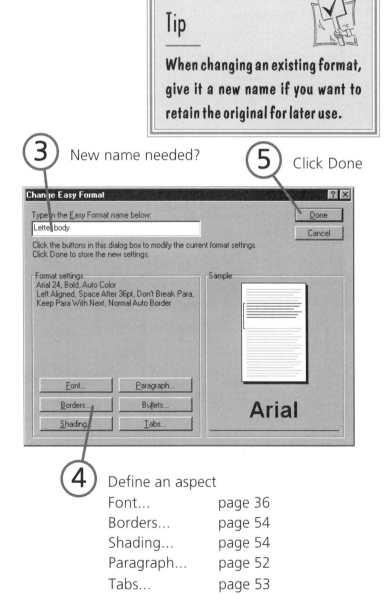

③ New name needed?

⑤ Click Done

④ Define an aspect

Font...	page 36
Borders...	page 54
Shading...	page 54
Paragraph...	page 52
Tabs...	page 53

Indents and Alignment

The Paragaph... dialog box gives you a one-stop method of setting the layout of text – its alignment, indents from the margins and spacing between lines.

● Indents (pushing text in from the margins) can be set from the ruler, and alignments from toolbar buttons, but it is only in the box that you can set indents really accurately.

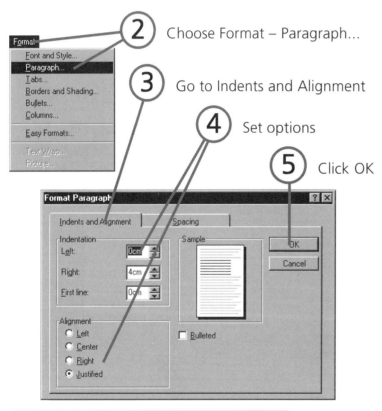

Choose Format – Paragraph...

Go to Indents and Alignment

Set options

Click OK

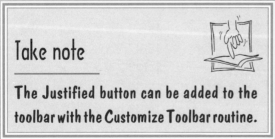

Take note

The Justified button can be added to the toolbar with the Customize Toolbar routine.

1 Select the paragraphs, or place the cursor to format new text.

2 Open the **Format** menu and select **Paragraph...**

3 At the **Paragraph** dialog box, switch to **Indents and Alignment**

4 Set the options.

5 Click [OK] when you have done.

❑ **Alignments**

Left ▤ alignment is the default. Lines start flush on the left, but have ragged right edges.

Fully justified ▤ text aligns with both margins. This gives a crisp right edge, but can produce big gaps between words.

Centre ▥ alignment is good for titles and special effects, but does not make for easy reading.

Use **Right** ▤ alignment for addresses, dates and other headings.

Basic steps

1 If the **Ruler** is not visible, open the **View** menu and click on **Ruler**.

❑ **To set the Right indent**

Point anywhere on the right triangle and drag it into position.

❑ **To set the Left indent**

Point at the *lower* left triangle and drag.

❑ **To set the First line indent**

Point at the *upper* left triangle and drag.

Indents

The width of lines of text can be controlled by both Margins and Indents.

● **Margins** are printer settings and controlled by the Page Setup routines. (See page 46.).

● **Indents** push the text in further from the margins, and are used to pick out paragraphs, for emphasis.

Left and Right indents set the distance of all lines from the relevant margins.This paragraph has a left indent of 1.5cm, and a right indent of 1cm.

First line indent sets the difference between the first and later lines. It can be negative – left of the left indent – to create a **hanging indent**, as here.

Indents can be set most accurately by typing values into the **Indents and Alignments** page of the **Paragraph** dialog box, but much of the time it is simpler to use the indent marker triangles on the ruler.

Left margin

Right margin

First line indent   Left indent   Right indent

The guide line appears as you drag on an indent marker

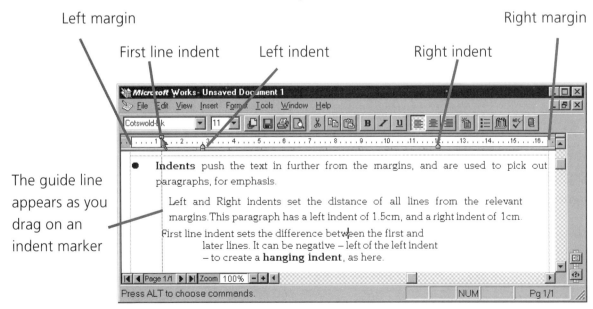

Breaks and Spacing

Breaks refers to what happens to paragraphs at the bottom of a page. Works will normally print as many lines as fit neatly on the page – not worrying about awkward breaks in mid-paragraph. If you want to ensure that a paragraph stays intact, even though it may mean a large gap at the bottom of a page, then set the **Don't break paragraph** option for it.

Spacing

For most purposes, it is enough to be able to switch between single-line spacing and double-spacing. Double-spacing can be used for emphasis, though **bold**, *italics* or larger text will do that better. It is best kept for those times when you want to leave space between lines for people to write notes or corrections.

Single ▭ and double space ▭ buttons can be added to the toolbar. You will find them in the Format set in the Customize Toolbar dialog box.

Basic steps

1 Select the paragraphs.

2 Open the **Format – Paragraph** dialog box, and switch to **Spacing**.

3 Use the arrows or type the number to set spacing in lines

4 Press **[Enter]** after typing a value or click ▭ OK ▭ to exit

Tip

If you have a list of items, or a set of short points, one to a line, these count as separate paragraphs. To keep them together, select them all and set the *Keep paragraph with next* option.

③ Use the arrows or type a value

② Open the Spacing tab

How should paragraphs break?

④ Click OK

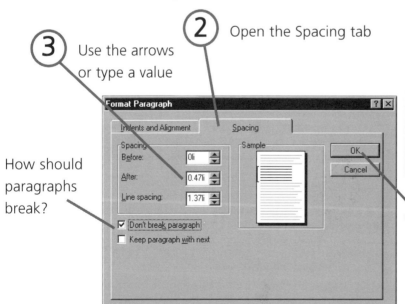

Basic steps

1 Select the block in which you want tabs.

2 If you have added the tabs buttons, and want a type other than left, click on its button.

3 Click on the Ruler to place a tab, dragging it into position.

❏ **To change the type or add leader dots**

4 Open the **Format** menu and select **Tabs....**

5 Pick the tab and set its alignment and leader.

6 Click [Set] to store its settings.

7 Return to 5 to adjust another tab.

8 Click [OK] when all are done.

❏ To remove unwanted tabs, drag them down off the ruler, or use the [Clear] button

Setting left tabs is simple – just click on the ruler. For centre, right and decimal tabs you must either bring their buttons onto the toolbar, or use the Tabs... dialog box. This is also used for setting leader dots or lines.

Centre	Left	Right	Decimal
WT1	Widget, large 94		7.99
WT2	Widget, small 15		3.99
GD	Gadget 44		11.49
GMB3	Gimble 5		1,029.99

① Select the text

③ Click on the ruler

② Select the type

⑧ Click OK

⑤ Pick a tab then adjust the settings

⑥ Click Set

Borders and Shading

If you want to place lines anywhere around a block of text, or borders around the whole page, use **Format – Borders and Shading...**

Use lines above or below paragraphs to mark off sections.

| Lines on either side can help to emphasise a block of text. |

Lines all around create a solid box. This can work well around the title on the front page of a report.

To make a box narrower, or pull in the side lines, select the paragraph and drag the indent markers inwards.

- ❑ **Text borders**
1. Select the paragraphs to be bordered.
2. Right click for the short menu and select **Borders and Shading...**
3. Go to the **Borders** tab.
4. Set the **Line Style**, and **Color**, if appropriate.
5. If you do not want a border all round, tick the sides to have lines in the **Border** area.
- ❑ **Page borders**
6. Switch to the **Page** tab.
7. Set the **Line Style** and **Color**
8. Set the **Distance from page edge** – you may have to change the Margins in Page Setup.

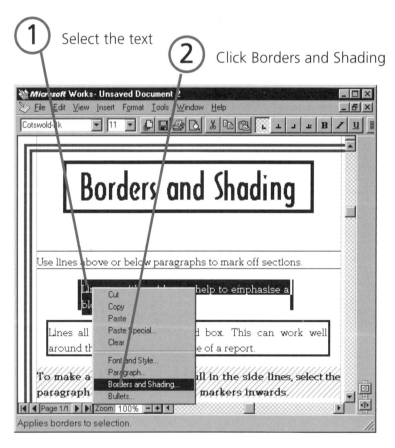

① Select the text

② Click Borders and Shading

Take note

You can also reach **Borders and Shading...** through the **Format** menu.

54

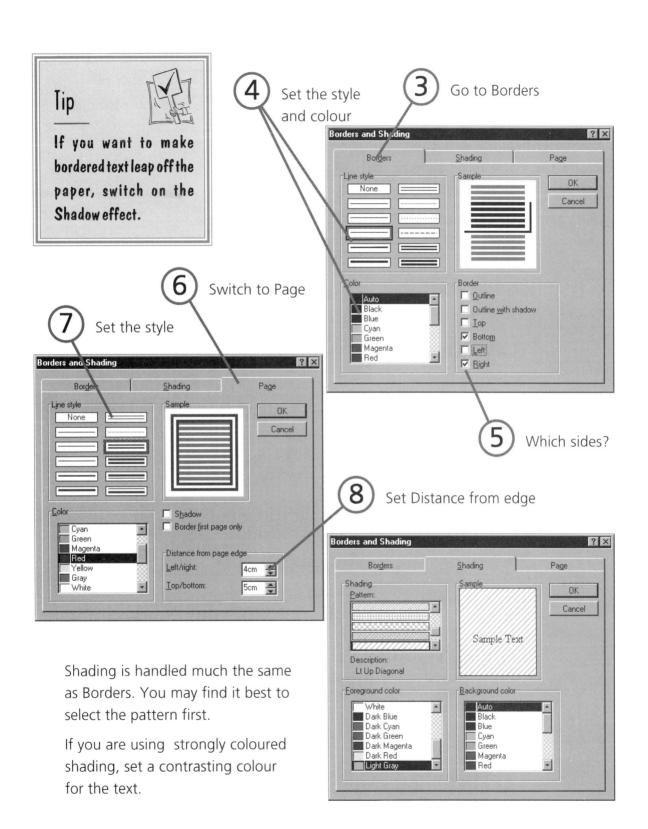

④ Set the style and colour

③ Go to Borders

⑥ Switch to Page

⑦ Set the style

⑤ Which sides?

⑧ Set Distance from edge

Shading is handled much the same as Borders. You may find it best to select the pattern first.

If you are using strongly coloured shading, set a contrasting colour for the text.

Headers and footers

Basic steps

Headers and footers , if defined, will appear at the top and bottom of every page. You can write into them the report title, chapter heading or author, and insert the current date and time, the page number and filename. These insertions are managed and kept up to date by Works.

Headers and footers are best tackled in Page Layout view – in Normal view they are both pushed up together at the very top of the file.

You can use the normal range of formatting and alignment on headers and footers.

1 Open the **View** menu and switch to **Page Layout**

2 Click the cursor into the Header or Footer.

3 Type in the text that you want to appear on each page.

Inserting items

4 Place the cursor where the item is to go.

5 Right click and select the item from the short menu.

(1) Use Page Layout View

You can use these to move into the Header or Footer

(2) Click into Header

(3) Type your text

(4) Place the cursor

(5) Select item to Insert

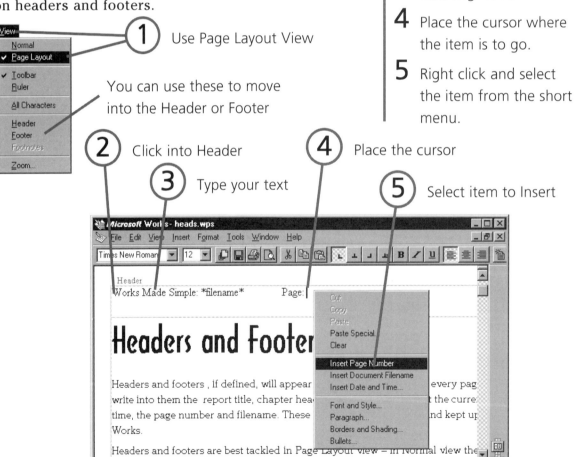

6 Choose a format and Insert

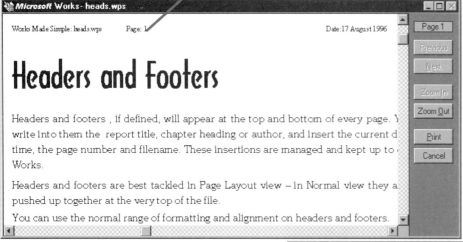

6 With **Date and Time**, choose a format in the dialog box, then click **Insert**

7 Select and format the header/footer as required.

7 Set fonts and styles

Headers and footers are usually set smaller than body text

Works Made Simple: heads.wps   Page: 1   Date:17 August 1996

Headers and Footers

Headers and footers , if defined, will appear at the top and bottom of every page. Y write into them the report title, chapter heading or author, and insert the current d time, the page number and filename. These insertions are managed and kept up to Works.

Headers and footers are best tackled in Page Layout view – in Normal view they a pushed up together at the very top of the file.

You can use the normal range of formatting and alignment on headers and footers.

❑ If you don't want Headers or Footers on the first (title?) page, go to **Page Setup**, switch to the **Other Options** tab and turn on the **No header (footer) on first page** option

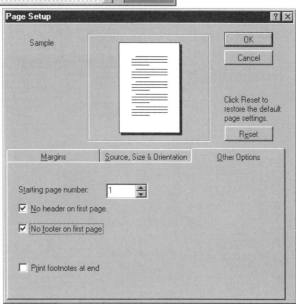

Columns

Use a multiple column layout where you want to have a number of separate stories on a page, or where a report is broken down into a set of distinct, headed paragraphs, perhaps interspersed with graphics.

Short paragraphs, that cover only a couple of lines across the full width of the page, will take 6 or 8 lines in columns. These solid blocks of text look more balanced and are easier to read.

You would normally want two or three columns on an A4 page – with four or more, the columns are too narrow, unless you are using a very small point size. Anything less than three or four words to a line looks far too scrappy.

1 Open the **Format** menu and select **Columns...**

2 At the dialog box, set the **Number of columns** and the **Space between** them.

3 Check **Lines between** if you want them. These will not be visible during editing, but are applied at print time.

4 Click [OK].

5 Start typing and leave Works to flow the text into the columns.

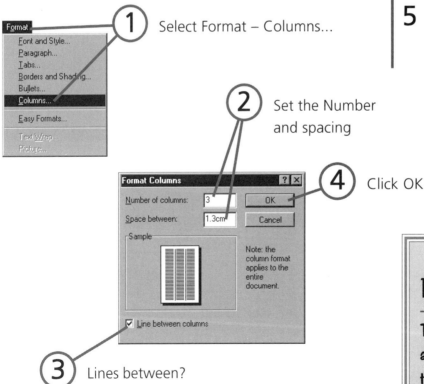

① Select Format – Columns...

② Set the Number and spacing

④ Click OK

③ Lines between?

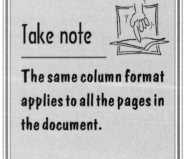

Take note

The same column format applies to all the pages in the document.

Text can only be written inside the columns, but if you want headlines across the page, insert Word Art text. At first, this will be squeezed into a single column. To spread it across the columns use the *Absolute* Text Wrap setting. (See *Word Art*, page 128.)

Short items can be picked out by dropping a border round them. This does not work as well in a full-width layout.

Short paragraphs work better in columns

Columns

Where?

Use a multiple column layout where you want to have a number of separate stories on a page, or where a report is broken down into a set of distinct, headed paragraphs, perhaps interspersed with graphics.

Chunkier text

Short paragraphs, that cover only a couple of lines across the full width of the page, will take 6 or 8 lines in columns. These solid blocks of text look more balanced and are easier to read.

Flexibility

With a three-column page, you have flexibility in placing graphics. Small ones can fit in one column, while larger ones can be spread over two or three.

Boxed items

Short items can be picked out by dropping a border round them. This does not work as well in a full-width layout.

How?

Simple. Just select the Column format and tell Works how many columns you want on a page. You want two or three columns on an A4 page. With four, the columns are too narrow, unless you are using a very small point size. Anything less than three or four words to a line looks far too scrappy.

Headlines

Text can only be written inside columns, but if you want headlines across the page, you can insert Word Art. (See *Word Art*).

All the Same

If you decide to use columns, the format applies to every page in the document.

Columns

Columns

Short paragraphs work better in columns

Word Art can also be used for captions across the columns

With a three-column page, you have flexibility in placing graphics. Small ones can fit in one column, while larger ones can be spread over two or three.

Printing

Page Layout view and the Print Preview facility give you a good idea of how the document will appear, but you can never be entirely sure until you see the printed copy. Some fonts do not come out quite the same on paper as on screen; grey shades become dot patterns; colours are never quite the same. If you have a long document, it is often worth printing a couple of sample pages, and checking those, before committing the whole lot to paper.

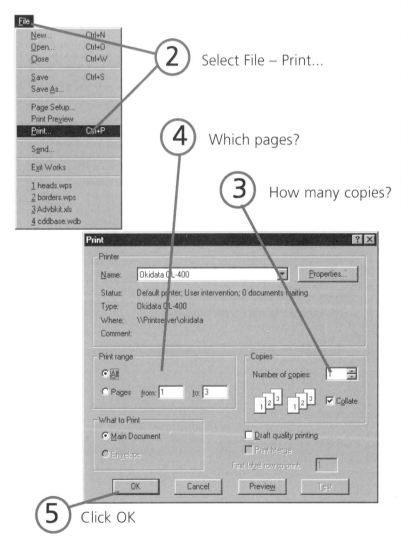

② Select File – Print...

④ Which pages?

③ How many copies?

⑤ Click OK

❑ **Quick printing**

1 If you don't want to change any of the current print settings, just or click 🖫 on the toolbar.

❑ **Controlled printing**

2 Open the **File** menu and select **Print**.

3 Set the **Number of Copies**.

4 Set the **Page Range**, specifying **Start** and **End** pages, or **All**.

5 Click ▢ OK ▢

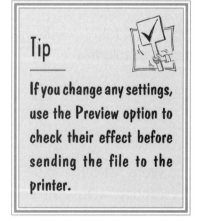

Tip

If you change any settings, use the Preview option to check their effect before sending the file to the printer.

60

Basic steps

Printer setup

1 Open the **File** menu and select **Print...**

2 If you are switching to another printer, select it from the list.

3 If you want to adjust the print settings, click

[Properties...]

❑ Every printer has its own Properties dialog box, but all should give you some control over the quality of print and graphics.

Works runs through Windows, and the Printer Setup routines that you will have done there, will be in place for your Works printing. As a result, you will probably find that you only have to bother with this on rare occasions. Use Setup when you want to switch to a second printer, or print sideways, or adjust the quality of the print.

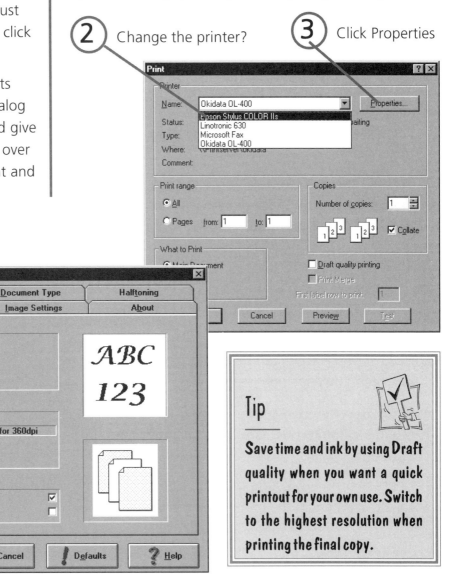

② Change the printer?

③ Click Properties

Tip

Save time and ink by using **Draft** quality when you want a quick printout for your own use. Switch to the highest resolution when printing the final copy.

Summary

❑ Use the **Page Setup** routines to set the paper size, orientation and margins.

❑ Use the Print Preview to see how your layout will look on paper.

❑ **Easy Formats** give you a quick way to put a professional gloss on your documents.

❑ **Indents, Alignment** and **Tabs** can be set from the ruler or toolbar buttons, though you may have to use the dialog boxes to get fine control.

❑ **Tabs** are easily set via the Ruler, but for more accurate positioning you should use the **Format Tabs** dialog box.

❑ You can control how paragraphs behave at page **Breaks** and set the **Spacing** between lines and between paragraphs.

❑ **Borders** can be added to any or all of the edges of a selected block of text, or to the whole page.

❑ You can use patterned and coloured **Shading** to highlight blocks of text.

❑ **Headers** and **Footers** can be added. You can insert into them the page number, filename and date, if wanted.

❑ Multiple **columns** offer a number of advantages for newsletters and certain types of reports.

❑ Check the settings before printing. If required, you can adjust them in the **printer's Properties** dialog box.

5 Working with numbers

Cells and contents

A spreadsheet is a grid of cells into which text, numbers and formulae can be written. With the Works spreadsheet, you also have control of fonts, lines and background patterns to enhance the appearance, so that, for example, the spreadsheet that calculates the blls can also produce professional-looking invoices. Where the spreadsheet is being used to analyse cash flows, departmental budgets or other sets of values that change over time or category, the easy chart-drawing routines can make the patterns of change more visible.

Two layers

With a word processor document, what you see is what you get. Spreadsheets are different. The text, numbers and formulae that are held in the cells are not necessarily what you see on screen. With formulae, the results are displayed; text items that are longer than the width of the cell will be clipped short if there is something in the cell to the right; numbers will appear as a set of # if they are too large to fit in a cell.

Entering and editing data

Entering data into a spreadsheet is significantly different from entering it into a word processor. Everything goes in through the Formula line, where the system checks it to see if it is a piece of text, a number or a formula – for these are each treated differently. The Formula line is linked to the current cell. It displays whatever is in the cell at the moment, and anything entered into the formula line is transferred to the cell.

Basic steps

❏ **To enter data**

1 Point at the target cell and click on it to make it current.

2 Start to type. The characters will appear in the formula line.

3 Use the [Left] / [Right] arrow keys to move along the line; [Back-space] or [Delete] to erase errors.

4 Click ☑ or press [Enter] when you have done. The display version of the data will appear in the cell.

❏ **To edit cell contents**

1 Make the target cell current.

2 Click in the Formula line, or press [F2] to start editing.

3 Click ☑ or press [Enter] to accept the changes. Click ☒ or press [Escape] to abandon

Jargon

Current cell – the last one you clicked with the mouse. It is marked by double-line borders.

Cell reference – a Column letter/Row number combination that identifies a cell. In the diagram, the current cell is C12 (Column C, Row 12).

Range – a set of cells, which may be one or more full rows or columns, or a block somewhere in the middle of the sheet.

Formula line – the slot at the top. Its contents are transferred to the current cell when you press [Enter]. All data is entered into cells through this line.

Wide text will flow over into empty cells.

Column letters

Formula line

Fonts and Formats

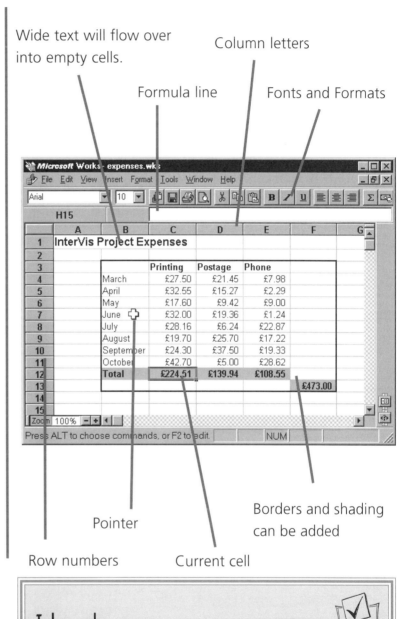

Row numbers

Pointer

Current cell

Borders and shading can be added

Take note

Works spreadsheet has 256 columns and 16,384 rows – that's a total of 4,194,304 cells! Big enough for you?

Selecting cells and ranges

Once you have selected a cell, or a range of cells, you can:

- apply a font style or alignment;
- add a border to some or all of its edges;
- erase its contents;
- use its references in a formula.
- move it to another position;

If you have to type a range reference, it is made up of the cell references of the top left and bottom right corners. Most of the time you will be able to get the references by selecting the range with the mouse.

Basic steps

❑ **To select a block**

1 Point to the top left cell (or any corner).

2 Hold down the mouse button and drag the highlight over the block.

❑ **To select a set of rows**

1 Point to the row number at the top or bottom of the set.

2 Drag up or down over the numbers to highlight the rows you want.

Block references shown here

① Start here

② Drag to the opposite corner

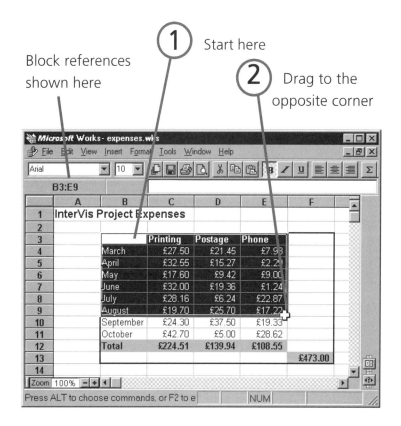

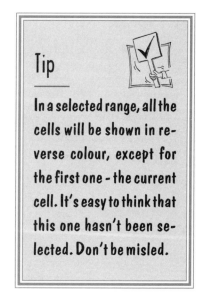

Tip

In a selected range, all the cells will be shown in reverse colour, except for the first one - the current cell. It's easy to think that this one hasn't been selected. Don't be misled.

❏ **To select a set of columns**

1 Point to the column letter at one end of the set.

2 Drag across the top of the columns to include the ones you want.

❏ **To select all cells**

1 Click on the top left corner, where the row and column headers meet,

or

open the **Edit** menu and choose **Select All**.

Note the reference

Click here to select all

① Point to a letter

② Drag across the top

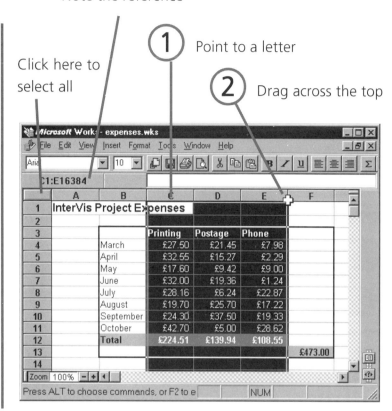

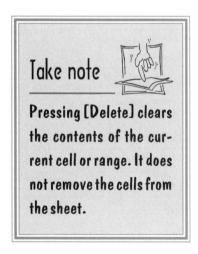

Take note

Pressing [Delete] clears the contents of the current cell or range. It does not remove the cells from the sheet.

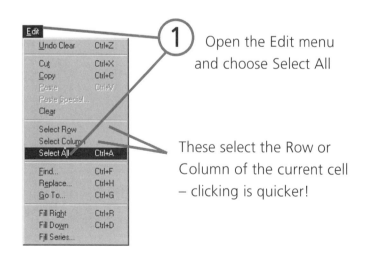

① Open the Edit menu and choose Select All

These select the Row or Column of the current cell – clicking is quicker!

Fonts and formats

Setting font types, styles and sizes for text is exactly the same here as it is in the word processor. Just select the block to be restyled and click a toolbar button or use the **Format | Font and Style** dialog box.

Number formats are a different matter. The way in which we write a number depends upon what it represents. If it is a money value, we would write a £ sign before and show two figures after the decimal point; with a large number, we would put commas every three digits to make it easier to read; if it is a percent, we place a % sign after it.

Works knows about all this. It can display numbers in different formats, and can understand numbers that are written in different formats. Type in £12,345.67 and it will realise that the underlying number is 12345.67, and also that you want to display it as currency. Type in 50% and it will store it as 0.5, while showing 50% on screen. Type in 0181-123 4567 and it will not be fooled into thinking its a sum – this gets treated as text. Try it and see for yourself.

Basic steps

1 Select the range of cells to be formatted.

2 Open the **Format** menu and select **Number...**

3 Select a **Format** from the panel on the left.

4 Set the number of decimal places.

5 With *Currency* values, you may want to use the **Negative numbers in red** option.

6 Check the Sample and adjust the options as required.

7 Click ☐ OK

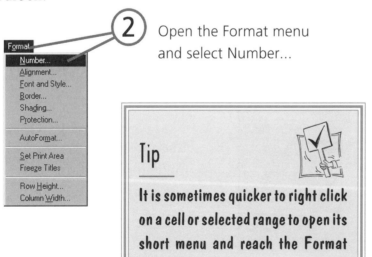

Open the Format menu and select Number...

Tip

It is sometimes quicker to right click on a cell or selected range to open its short menu and reach the Format dialog box from there.

Take note

The Currency button is part of the standard toolbar set. Buttons can be added for Comma and Percent.

General is the default – numbers appear as they were written.

Currency 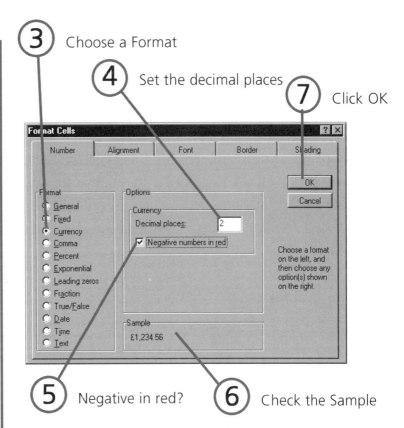 places a £ at the front, commas every 3 digits.

Commas places a comma every 3 digits.

Percent multiplies the value by 100 and adds the % sign at the end.

Exponential is used for very large or very small numbers.

Fractions can sometimes be useful. Let it work out the closest fraction, or fix the denominator.

Text treats the digits as text, not as a value.

③ Choose a Format

④ Set the decimal places

⑦ Click OK

⑤ Negative in red?

⑥ Check the Sample

A small selection of the number formats that Works can handle. The number of decimal places can be set in any format. With Currency and Comma formats, you can have negative numbers shown in red.

If you see "######" increase the column width to display the number properly.

	A	B	C	D	E	F
1	General	Currency	Comma, 1DP	Percent. 0DP	Exponent, 6DP	Fraction
2	1	£1.00	1.0	100%	1.000000E+00	1
3	1.2	£1.20	1.2	120%	1.200000E+00	1 3/16
4	1.2345	£1.23	1.2	123%	1.234500E+00	1 1/4
5	1234	£1,234.00	1,234.0	123400%	1.234000E+03	1234
6	1234567	£1,234,567.00	1,234,567.0	123456700%	1.234567E+06	1234567
7	0.123	£0.12	0.1	12%	1.230000E-01	0 1/8
8	-12.3	-£12.30	-12.3	-1230%	-1.230000E+01	-12 5/16
9	123456789.9	£123,456,789.88	123,456,789.9	12345678988%	1.234568E+08	#########
10						

Microsoft Works- numbform.wks

File Edit View Insert Format Tools Window Help

F9   123456789.87654

Press ALT to choose commands, or F2 to edit.   NUM

Alignment

There are more alignment options in the Spreadsheet than in the Word Processor. **Left**, **Right** and **Centre** alternatives, which can be used to align text within cells, are available on the toolbar ▤▤▤. The **Format – Alignment** panel also has **Fill** and **Centre**, which align a single item of text within a set of cells, and **General**, which aligns text to the left and numbers to the right. This works well, though the headings of columns of numbers look better if they too are aligned to the right.

1 Select the range of cells to be aligned.

2 Open the **Format** menu and select **Alignment...**

3 Select a **Horizontal Alignment** option.

4 If you want to adjust the **Vertical** position of the text within the cell, set an option.

5 Click ▭ OK ▭.

① Select the block

② Open the Format menu and select Alignment...

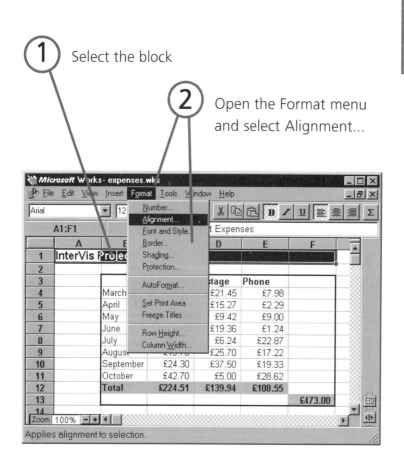

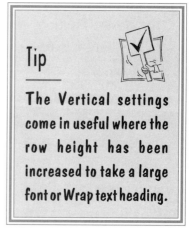

Tip

The Vertical settings come in useful where the row height has been increased to take a large font or Wrap text heading.

General aligns text to the left and numbers to the right.

Left, **Right** and **Centre** are the same as in the Word Processor.

Fill repeats whatever is in the first cell to fill the selected block. Use it to create dividing lines of characters.

Centre across selection takes whatever is in the first cell and positions it centrally in the selected block.

Wordwrap takes a long string of text and breaks it into multiple lines, to fit within the width of the cell. The row height will be increased to fit in the extra lines.

Vertical alignment set to Top
.

Wrap text

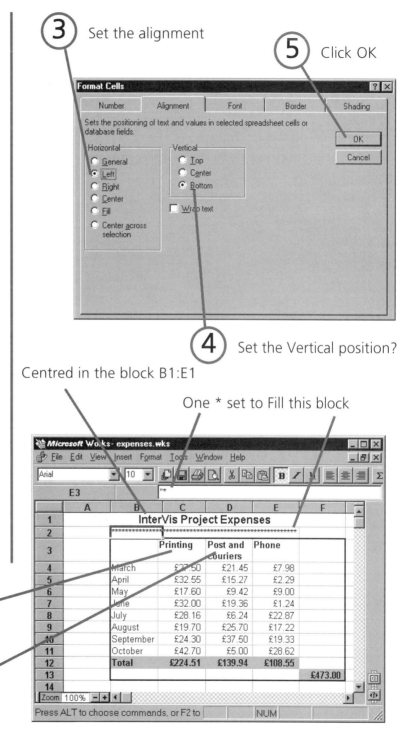

③ Set the alignment

⑤ Click OK

④ Set the Vertical position?

Centred in the block B1:E1

One * set to Fill this block

71

Borders and Shading

Borders can help to create a more visual structure to your sheet. Placed around a block, they will group the contents into one unit; placed along one side or beneath, they will separate values from their headings or totals.

Shaded and coloured backgrounds can focus your readers' attention on the most important aspects of the sheet – though some patterns can make the contents virtually unreadable. This may, or may not, be a bad thing.

Basic steps

❑ **To add borders**

1 Highlight the cells to be formatted.

2 Open the **Format** menu and select **Borders...**

3 Click on the **Borders** which are to be lined.

4 Select the **Line Style**, and **Colour** if wanted.

5 Click ▭ OK ▭.

❑ **To remove borders**

1 Highlight the cells to be tidied up.

2 Select the blank for the **Line Style**.

3 Click on the **Border** sides that you want to clear.

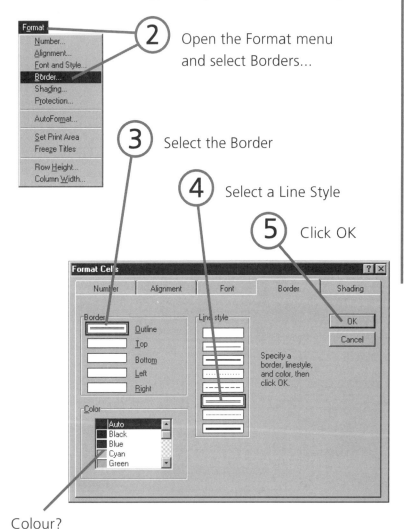

② Open the Format menu and select Borders...

③ Select the Border

④ Select a Line Style

⑤ Click OK

Colour?

Take note

Bug warning! Setting the Outside to blank does not remove lines. Set blanks for Top, Bottom, Left and Right to remove them all.

Basic steps

❑ **To use shading**

1 Highlight the cells to be formatted.

2 Open the **Format** menu and select **Shading...**

3 Pick a **Pattern** from the list.

4 Set **Foreground** and **Background** colours.

5 Check the **Sample**, and if you are happy, click [OK].

For coloured text, use Color option in the Font and Style dialog box.

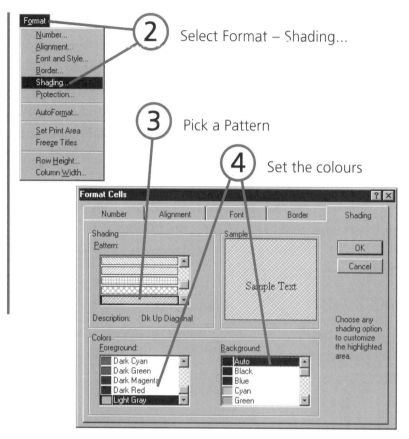

② Select Format – Shading...

③ Pick a Pattern

④ Set the colours

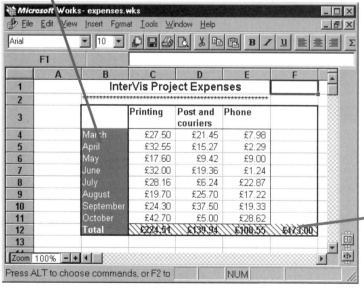

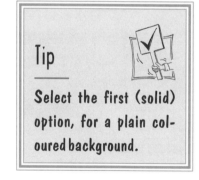

Tip

Select the first (solid) option, for a plain coloured background.

Patterns can make the contents unreadable

Autoformats

The spreadsheet's Autoformats, like the word processor's Easy Formats, offer an instant design solution for common situations. They are all based on headed tables or lists, but with 14 alternatives to choose from, you should find something there to suit most of your needs. The formatting includes that of the numbers, and the style of text, as well as shading and borders.

Colours and shades are best avoided if you are not using a colour printer, as they are likely to be translated into dot patterns, making text difficult to read.

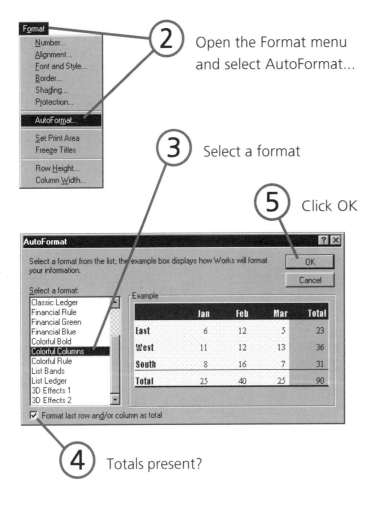

② Open the Format menu and select AutoFormat...

③ Select a format

⑤ Click OK

④ Totals present?

Basic steps

1 Select the table or list to be formatted, including its headers and totals.

2 From the **Format** menu select **AutoFormat...**

3 Pick a **format**, checking its appearance with the **Example**.

4 If it is not appropriate, turn off **Format last row and/or column as total**.

5 Click ☐ OK ☐.

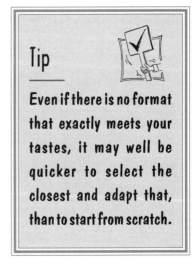

Tip

Even if there is no format that exactly meets your tastes, it may well be quicker to select the closest and adapt that, than to start from scratch.

74

Basic steps

Writing formulae

❏ To total a range

1 Click on the cell below the column (or to the right of the row).

2 Click on the Σ *Autosum* button.

3 You will see that the column (or row) is highlighted, and that there is =SUM(*range*) in the formula line.

4 If range covers the right cells, click ✔ or press **[Enter]** to accept the formula.

You won't get far with a spreadsheet without writing formulae, but at least Works makes it a fairly painless business. If you just want to total a column or row of figures, it only takes a click of a button with **Autosum**. Other calculations take a little more effort, but point and click references, and readily-accessible lists of functions simplify the process and reduce the chance of errors.

A formula starts with the = sign and can contain a mixture of cell or range references, numbers, text and functions, joined by operators. These include the arithmetic symbols **/*-+^** and a few others.

Examples of simple formulae:

= 4 * C1   4 times the contents of cell C1

= B3+B4   the value in B3 added to that in B4

=SUM(A5:A12) the sum of the values in cells A5 to A12.

References can be typed into the formula line, or pulled in by clicking on a cell or highlighting a range.

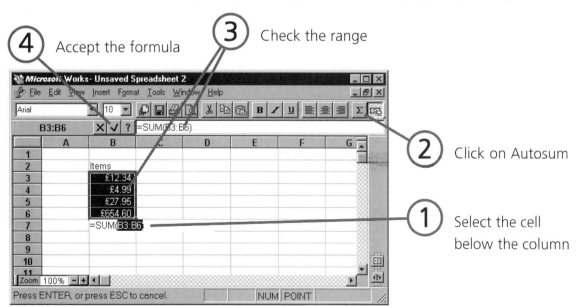

④ Accept the formula

③ Check the range

② Click on Autosum

① Select the cell below the column

Basic steps

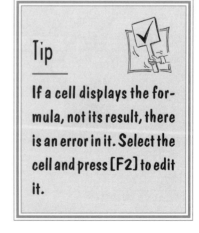

❑ **To write a formula**

1 Click on the cell where the formula is to go.

2 Type **=**

3 Type the number, or point and click to get a cell reference.

4 Type an operator symbol **/*-+**

5 Type the next number, or select the next reference.

6 Repeat steps 4 and 5, as necessary, to complete the formula.

7 Click **✓** or press [Enter].

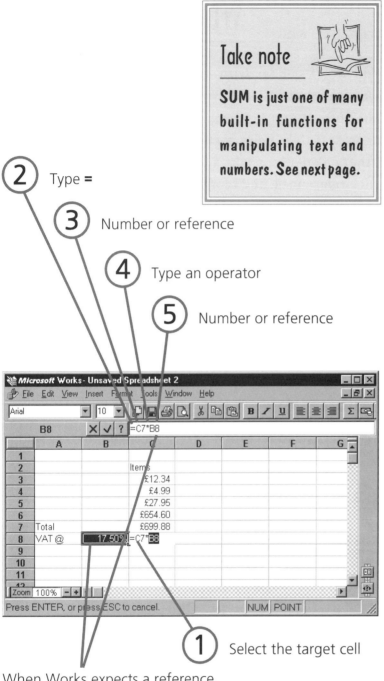

② Type **=**

③ Number or reference

④ Type an operator

⑤ Number or reference

① Select the target cell

When Works expects a reference, clicking on a cell writes the reference into the formula

Basic steps

❑ **To name a range**

1 Select the cell or the range.

2 Open the **Insert** menu and select **Range Name..**

3 Type a suitable name into the top slot.

4 Click [OK].

❑ **To remove a name**

1 Open the **Insert** menu and select **Range Name...**

2 Highlight the name in the list.

3 Click [Delete].

Cell and range references are hard to remember, and if you reorganise the layout of the spreadsheet, you may have to learn them all again. To make life simpler, Works allows you to give meaningful names to cells and ranges. Use them. They will make your formulae more readable, and if you want to transfer data into a word processed document, you can only do this with named ranges.

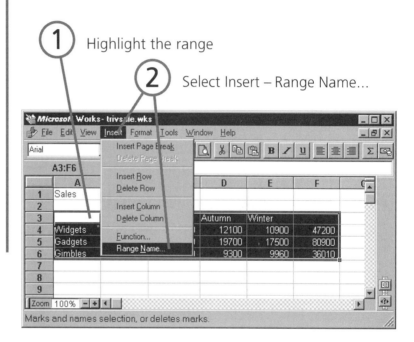

① Highlight the range

② Select Insert – Range Name...

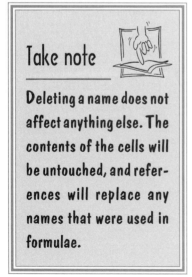

Take note

Deleting a name does not affect anything else. The contents of the cells will be untouched, and references will replace any names that were used in formulae.

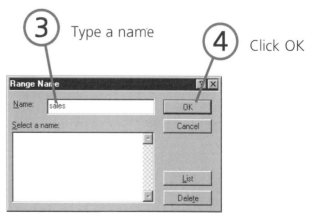

③ Type a name

④ Click OK

Functions

A function takes one or more number or text values, performs some kind of process on them and gives a new value in return. It may be a simple process, as with SUM, which adds up a range of numbers. It may be a familiar one such as SIN, which gives the sine of an angle. It may be a complex process that you wouldn't meet anywhere except on a spreadsheet. PMT, for example, will give you the regular repayment on a mortgage. There is no room here to look at these functions properly, but what we can do is cover the basics of how to use them.

All functions come with dummy arguments in their brackets, e.g. SIN(x) or COUNT(RangeRef0,RangeRef1,...). These tell you the type of values that you should be supplying to the function. Replace the dummies with suitable cell or range references, and the function is ready to roll.

The most common dummy arguments are:

> x standing for a number or the reference of a cell that contains a number

> *RangeRef0* to be replaced by a range reference

> ... indicates that you can repeat the last type of value. For example, COUNT(RangeRef0,RangeRef1,...) tells you how many cells in one or more ranges contain something. It could be written:

> COUNT(A2:A12) for one partial column

> COUNT(A1:E12) for one block

> COUNT(A2:A12, E5:H10) counting two ranges.

1 Select the cell into which the formula should go.

2 Open the **Insert** menu and select **Function...** or click the Insert Function =f(x) button, if you have added it to your toolbar.

3 Pick the **Category** of function from the panel on the left.

4 Scroll through the list to find the one you want, and click on it.

5 Click [Insert] to copy it to the formula line.

6 Replace the dummy argument(s) with suitable values or references.

7 Enter the formula.

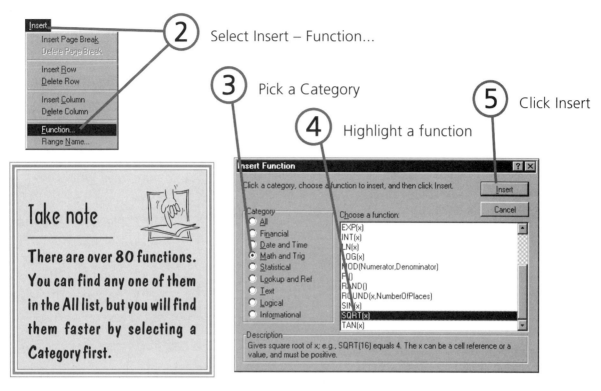

② Select Insert – Function...

③ Pick a Category

④ Highlight a function

⑤ Click Insert

Take note

There are over 80 functions. You can find any one of them in the All list, but you will find them faster by selecting a Category first.

Insert Function

Click a category, choose a function to insert, and then click Insert.

Insert

Cancel

Category
- All
- Financial
- Date and Time
- Math and Trig
- Statistical
- Lookup and Ref
- Text
- Logical
- Informational

Choose a function:
EXP(x)
INT(x)
LN(x)
LOG(x)
MOD(Numerator,Denominator)
PI()
RAND()
ROUND(x,NumberOfPlaces)
SIN(x)
SQRT(x)
TAN(x)

Description
Gives square root of x; e.g., SQRT(16) equals 4. The x can be a cell reference or a value, and must be positive.

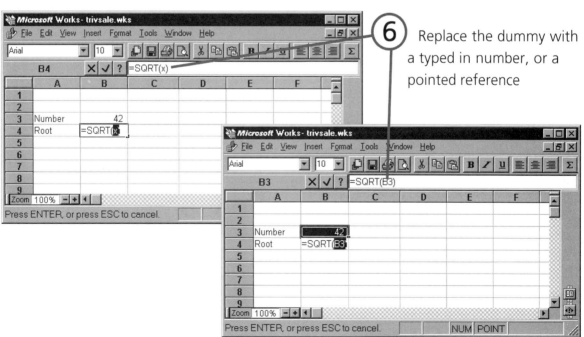

⑥ Replace the dummy with a typed in number, or a pointed reference

79

Lookup functions

One category of functions that are worth exploration are the Lookup functions. They can be really useful, and in getting to grips with these you will master most of the techniques you need for working with other functions.

A Lookup function will scan through a list of items in a table, to find a key item, then pick a value out of the corresponding place in another list within the table. The example opposite shows a simple price and stock list being used by two Lookup formulae. When an item's name is typed into a key cell, the functions scan the list and pick out its price and stock level.

Basic steps

❑ **To use VLOOKUP**

1 Create a table of data, with index values on the left.

2 Pick a cell into which you will write the key value and type in something which is in the table. This will test the formulae.

3 Select the cell which will hold the formula.

① Create a table of values

② Type a test value into a cell

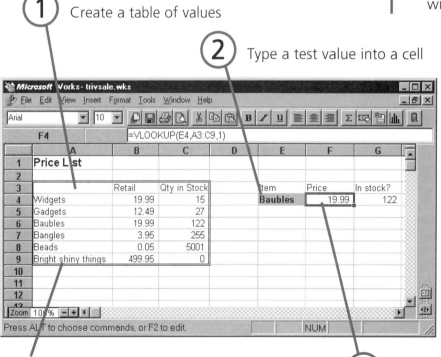

③ Go to the formula's cell

The key items – the ones to be matched by the Lookup function – must be in the first column. The values to be looked up are in columns to its right.

4 Call up the **Insert Function...** dialog box.

5 Click on the **Lookup and Ref** category, select **VLOOKUP**.

6 Click [Insert] to copy it into the formula line.

7 The *LookupValue* will be highlighted. Select the cell containing your key value to replace this dummy with the reference.

8 Highlight *RangeRef*, then select the range that covers the table.

9 Delete *ColNum* and type 1 to get the value from the first column to the right of the index values, or 2 to get the value in the second column.

10 Click ✓ to accept the formula.

There are two similar functions.

● **HLOOKUP** works with tables where the index values are written across the top of the table;

● **VLOOKUP** expects the index values to be down the left side fo the table.

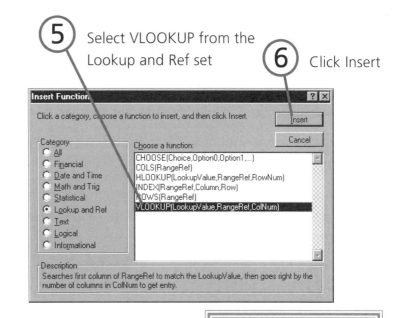

⑤ Select VLOOKUP from the Lookup and Ref set

⑥ Click Insert

=VLOOKUP(E4,**RangeRef**,ColNum)

After the first dummy, you will have to highlight the dummies yourself before you can replace them with a pulled-in reference.

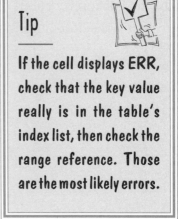

Tip

If the cell displays ERR, check that the key value really is in the table's index list, then check the range reference. Those are the most likely errors.

Summary

❑ A spreadsheet is a grid of **cells**, each identified by its **row** and **column reference**. A cell's contents and its screen display may differ. Formulae are shown by their resulting values; text may be cropped short and numbers shown as hashes in a narrow column.

❑ Rows and columns can be **selected** by their header numbers and letters; blocks are selected by dragging a highlight from one corner to the opposite one.

❑ The appearance of the sheet can be enhanced by the use of **fonts**, **alignments**, **borders** and **shading**.

❑ **Numbers** can be displayed in different formats.

❑ The **Autoformat** options provide a quick way to give a professional finish to tables.

❑ **Formulae** all start with = and may include a mixture of text and number values, cell and range reference and functions.

❑ There is a wide range of **functions**, organised into several categories. They are easily accessed through the **Insert Function** dialog box.

❑ The **Lookup** functions allow you to write formulae that will extract information from a table.

6 Working with tables

Copying and filling

The usual **Edit Copy**, **Cut** and **Paste** facilities are available here, as anywhere else in Windows, but there are also alternatives which may be better. Much of your copying is likely to be of formulae to create a table. For this, the **Fill Right** and **Fill Down** commands are quicker and simpler. They will take the formula in the first cell of a range and copy it into all the other cells, adjusting the references as they go, so that the formulae continue to apply to the same relative cells.

For example, if you had a formula in C2 that read:

= A2 * B2

When this is copied down into C3, the formula will read:

= A3 * B3

As you would normally want the same type of formula all down the table, this automatic adjustment of references is generally a good thing.

① Write a formula in the top cell

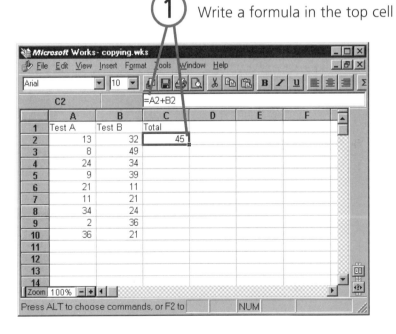

Basic steps

- ❏ **To Fill Down**

1 Write a formula in the cell at the top of the table.

2 Select the range, starting with your formula cell and continuing to the bottom of the table.

3 Open the **Edit** menu and select **Fill Down...** or click 🔽 if you have added it to the toolbar.

4 Check any of the new formulae and you should see that their references have been adjusted to suit their new positions.

Tip

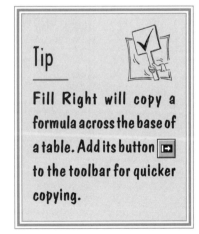

Fill Right will copy a formula across the base of a table. Add its button 🔁 to the toolbar for quicker copying.

Fixed references

You may want to copy a formula, but keep a references unchanged. For example, you might want to calculate the VAT on each item in a table, and the VAT rate is stored in one cell.

To keep a reference unchanged, edit the formula and type a $ sign before the column letter and row number.

If C1 held this:

   = A1 * B1

when copied into C2 it would read:

   = A2 * B1

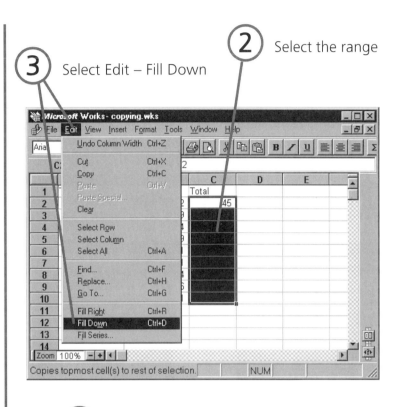

② Select the range

③ Select Edit – Fill Down

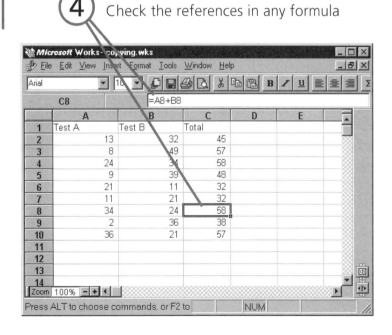

④ Check the references in any formula

Fill Series

The third option of this type, **Fill Series**, does not copy, but it does create a sequence of numbers or dates. When you are setting up a schedule of work, or any kind of numbered list, it can save a great deal of tedious typing. All the command needs is a starting number or date, and a place to put the series.

1 Type into the top or leftmost cell the first number or date.

2 Select the range which the series will occupy.

3 Open the **Edit** menu and select **Fill Series...** or click on ⊞ if you have added it to your toolbar.

4 At the dialog box, you will be offered a selection of intervals if you are working with dates. Click the **Unit** that you want.

5 Type in the **Step by** value.

6 Click [OK].

① Type the start value

③ Select Edit – Fill Series

② Select the range

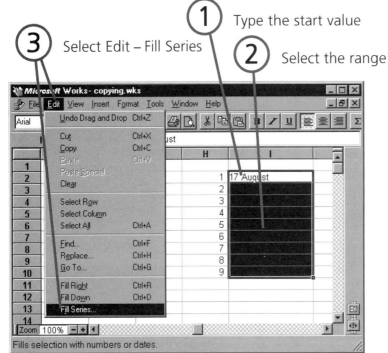

④ Pick a Unit

⑥ Click OK

⑤ Type the Step

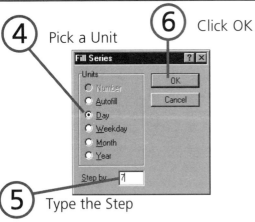

Take note

Works recognises dates in several styles. You can write 12th August 1996 as 07/12/96 (month first!) or 12 August 96 or 12 aug. They will all be taken to mean the same date. The display can be changed through the Format dialog box.

Cut and Paste Copying

1 Select the cell(s) to be copied.

2 Open the **Edit** menu and select **Copy**, or click on ▣

3 Select the range into which the cells are to be duplicated.

4 Open the **Edit** menu and select **Paste**, or click on ▣

If you want to copy formulae or data anywhere other than down or right, you must turn to the **Edit – Copy** and **Paste** commands.

For straightforward one-to-one copying, their use is exactly the same as elsewhere in Windows, but you are not limited to this. You can also do one-to-many copying – duplicating a formula throughout a range.

(1) Select the source cell

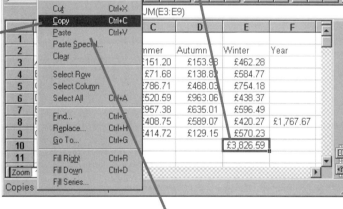

(2) Use Edit – Copy

(3) Select the target range

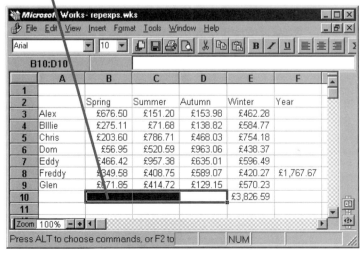

(4) Use Edit – Paste

Tip

Learn the shortcuts:

[Ctrl]-[X]	**Cut**
[Ctrl]-[C]	**Copy**
[Ctrl]-[V]	**Paste**

Heights and widths

The spreadsheet grid is not fixed. You can adjust the layout and the column widths and row heights. You can make them bigger to give more room for the contents of cells or to create more space between items, or smaller, to fit more on a page. You can even **hide** rows or columns by adjusting their heights and widths down to zero.

Height and width adjustments are essentially cosmetic. They may improve the presentation of the spreadsheet and make it easier to read, but they will not affect any of the underlying structure on calculations in any way.

□ **To adjust a single row**

1 Move the pointer to the dividing line **below** the row you want to adjust.

2 When the pointer changes to the ADJUST double arrow, hold down the mouse button and drag to the desired height.

□ **To adjust a single column**

1 Move the pointer to the dividing line **to the right** of the column you want to adjust.

2 Drag the ADJUST pointer to the desired width.

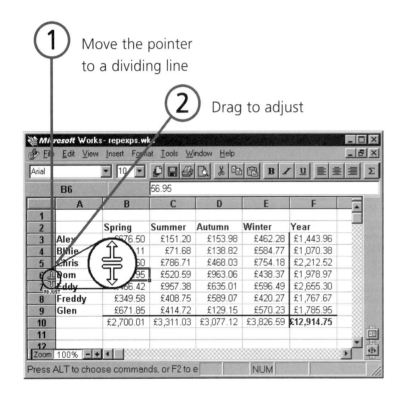

① Move the pointer to a dividing line

② Drag to adjust

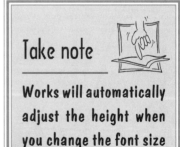

Take note

Works will automatically adjust the height when you change the font size of any cell in the row.

Basic steps

To adjust a set of columns

1 Select the columns by their letters, or select any block of cells that spans the set.

2 Open the **Format** menu or right click for the short menu and select **Column Width...**

3 Type in a new value in the dialog box. The range is from 0, which will hide them all, and 79, at which one column will fill the screen.

4 Click [OK].

To adjust a set of rows

1 Follow the steps above, but using the **Row Height...** command. Heights are given in point sizes. The default is 12 to fit 10 point text.

Multiple adjustments

Dragging the adjust pointer will only change the size of one row or column at a time. If you want to adjust the size of a set of them in one fell swoop, you must tackle it through the **Column Width** dialog box..

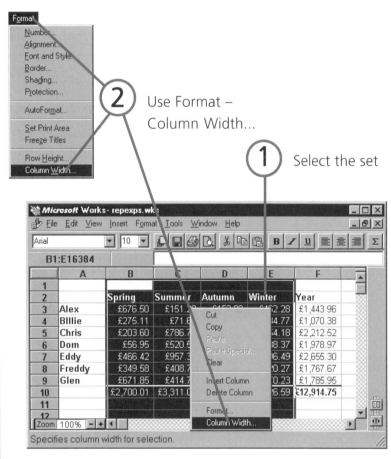

Use Format – Column Width...

① Select the set

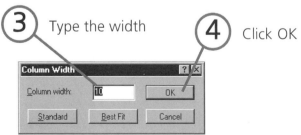

③ Type the width

④ Click OK

Hidden rows & columns

You may have a spreadsheet which contains confidential material, but which you want to be able to use it for public consumption. An invoicing sheet, for example, might have formulae and percentages to calculate your overheads. You want to print customers' copies from this sheet, but without revealing your secrets. The problem can be solved by hiding the rows or columns that contain the sensitive data. Of course, if you drag a height or width to zero by accident, the hiding becomes the problem!

To recover hidden rows and columns, you must first select them. You cannot do this with the mouse as you cannot see them. The only way is to use the **Go To** facility to leap to a cell in the hidden area. The height or width can then be restored via the **Format** menu.

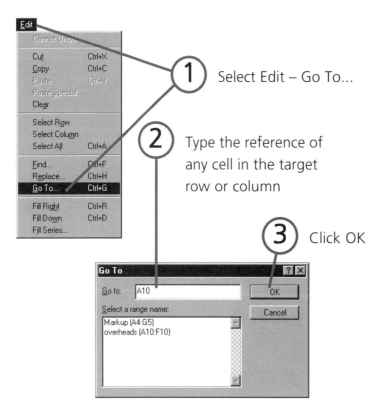

Select Edit – Go To...

Type the reference of any cell in the target row or column

Click OK

Basic steps

❑ **To hide rows or columns**

1 Drag the dividing line up or left until it meets the line on the opposite side of the row or column.

❑ **To restore hidden rows or columns**

1 Open the **Edit** menu and select **Go To**.

2 Type in the reference of any cell in the row.

3 Click OK.

4 By going to the cell, you have selected it, and its row or column. You can now use the **Format** menu to adjust the height or width. (See previous page.)

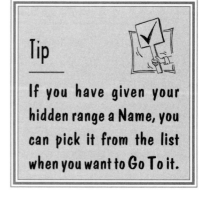

Tip

If you have given your hidden range a **Name**, you can pick it from the list when you want to **Go To** it.

90

Adjusting the layout

☐ **To move a row**

1 Click on the number to select the row.

2 Move the pointer into the grid area, near the bottom of the row.

3 When the pointer changes from the cross to the DRAG arrow, hold down the mouse button and move the row to its new place.

4 Release the button and the row will insert itself between the existing rows.

☐ **To move a column**

Follow the same steps as above, but look for the DRAG arrow by the right of the column.

The spreadsheet layout is not fixed. At any point you can move, insert or delete rows or columns, or move blocks of cells.

1 Select the whole row

2 Get the drag arrow

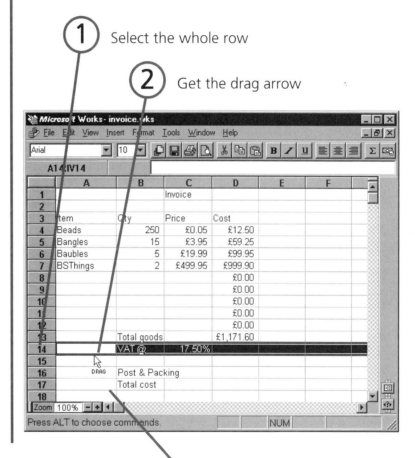

3 Pull to its new place

Take note

When you move any cells containing formulae, you may have to change their cell references for the formulae to continue to have the same effect.

Moving blocks

Moving blocks of cells is different from moving rows or columns. The process is the same, and cell references in formulae are adjusted in the same way, but the effects on the sheet are different.

When you move a full row or column into a new position, existing lines make space for it, and the hole that it left is closed up. When you move a block, you lift its data and formulae out of the cells and place them in the new location. A hole is left behind, and the moved contents will overwrite anything that was there before.

Basic steps

❑ **To move a block**

1 Select the block.

2 Place the cross pointer over any of the edges or corners to get the DRAG arrow.

3 Drag the outline to its new position, taking care not to overlap any wanted data.

4 Release to drop the block into its new position.

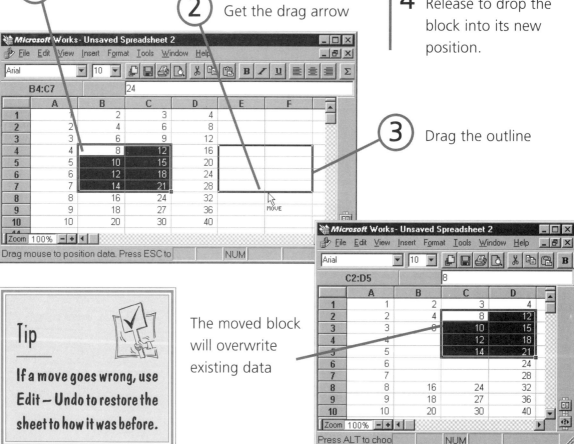

① Select the block

② Get the drag arrow

③ Drag the outline

The moved block will overwrite existing data

> **Tip**
>
> If a move goes wrong, use Edit – Undo to restore the sheet to how it was before.

92

Basic steps

Inserting and deleting

❏ **To insert rows or columns**

1 Select as many rows/ columns as you want to insert, at the place where you want them to go.

2 Right click for the short menu or open the **Insert** menu and select **Row/Column**. Existing rows will move down, columns move right to make room.

❏ **To delete rows or columns**

1 Select the rows/col- umns you want to delete.

2 Open short menu or the **Insert** menu and select **Delete Row/ Column**.

You can only insert or delete rows or columns, and not blocks within the sheet. Bear in mind that it is the *whole* row, or column, that is removed. If the occupied area of your sheet extends beyond the visible screen, check along the line to see if there is any data elsewhere that you would prefer not to lose.

There are optional buttons to cover all four insert/delete row/column combinations. If you have to do a major restructure of a sheet, add them to the toolbar.

 Insert row   **Delete row**

 Insert column   **Delete column**

① Mark where rows are to go

② Insert new rows

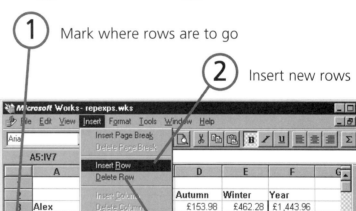

If a single cell or a block is selected when you open the menu, both Row and Column Insert and Delete commands are available.

Delete commands are also on the Insert menu

Sorting

Where you have a table of data organised, database-wise, so that each row holds details of one contact, customer, stock item or whatever, this can be sorted into order. The sort can be ascending or descending, numeric or alphabetic, and can be based on up to three columns. A contact list, for example, could be sorted first by County, then by Town and finally by Name.

Basic steps

1 Select the block to be sorted

2 Open the **Tools** menu and select **Sort...**

3 At the first dialog box, chose **Sort all the information** only if your database extends right across the sheet.

4 To sort on more than one column, click [Advanced...].

5 Pick the column on which to sort.

6 Choose the order – **Ascending** or **Descending.**

7 Repeat steps 5 and 6 for multi-column sorts.

8 If the selected block includes headings, set the **Header rows** option.

9 Click [Sort].

① Select the block of data to be sorted

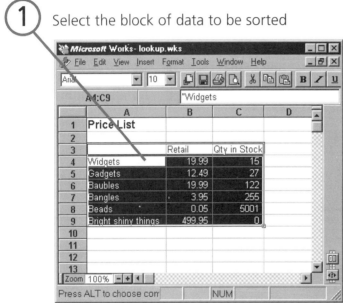

② Select Tools – Sort...

③ Sort the selected area only

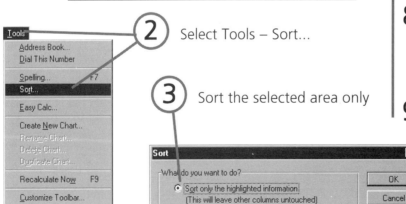

94

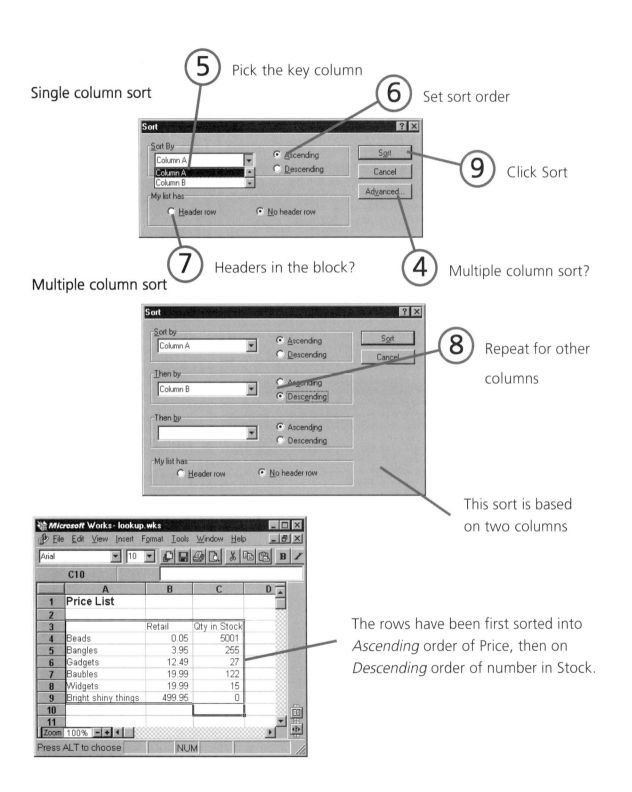

Single column sort

⑤ Pick the key column

⑥ Set sort order

⑨ Click Sort

⑦ Headers in the block?

④ Multiple column sort?

Multiple column sort

⑧ Repeat for other columns

This sort is based on two columns

The rows have been first sorted into *Ascending* order of Price, then on *Descending* order of number in Stock.

95

Charts from tables

Graphs and charts can bring out the underlying patterns in sets of numbers, and with Works you have a good range of charting styles, to cope with all kinds of data. Creating a chart could scarcely be simpler, and once created, a chart can easily be adapted. A few minutes' experimenting with different styles should be enough to find one that best displays the underlying patterns.

To create a chart, you must first have a table of figures. Works assumes that the table will have headings above and to the left, and that the data will be organised in rows. Works can also cope with other layouts, through its Advanced options.

Basic steps

1 Select the block of cells containing the figures and their headings.

2 Open the **Tools** menu and select **Create New Chart...** or click on the toolbar.

3 Pick the **Type** (N.B. It can be changed later.)

4 Add a **Title**, **Border** and **Gridlines** if wanted.

① Select the table   ② Create a New Chart

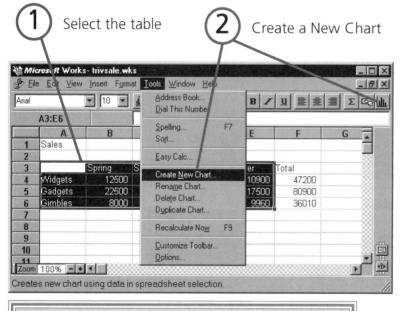

Tip

If you have several charts on one sheet, or if you want to insert charts later into a word processed document, give them meaningful names with Tools – Name Chart.

Take note

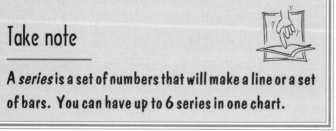

A *series* is a set of numbers that will make a line or a set of bars. You can have up to 6 series in one chart.

- ❑ If your table is non-standard...

5 Open the **Advanced Options** tab.

6 If your series run down the columns, click on the **Down** option.

7 If the First column does not contain headings, click on **Category**.

8 If the **First row** does not contain headings, click on **Y values**.

9 Click .

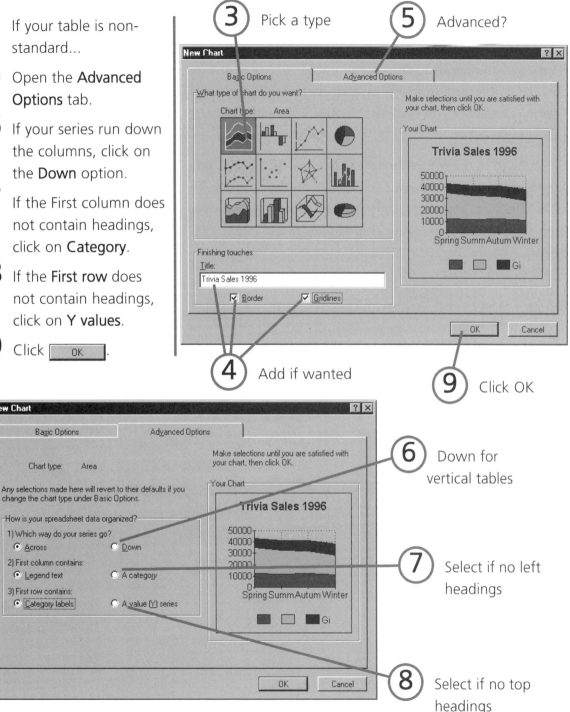

③ Pick a type

⑤ Advanced?

④ Add if wanted

⑨ Click OK

⑥ Down for vertical tables

⑦ Select if no left headings

⑧ Select if no top headings

Tailor-made charts

A chart appears in a window of its own, not within the spreadsheet, and when that window is on top, you will see a new set of buttons in the toolbar. Most of these are for selecting different chart types, and there is another new one that will take you back to the spreadsheet at the site of the first series.

If you want to make significant changes to the chart, you are best working through the Format menu options. To alter the font, style or other property of an individual item, right click on it for its short menu in the usual way.

❑ **To change patterns**

1 Open the **Format** menu and select **Shading and Color...**

2 Click the **Series** you want to reformat.

3 Select a fill or line **Color** and a **Pattern**.

4 Click [Format] to fix your choices.

5 Repeat steps 2 to 4 for each series.

6 **Close** the dialog box.

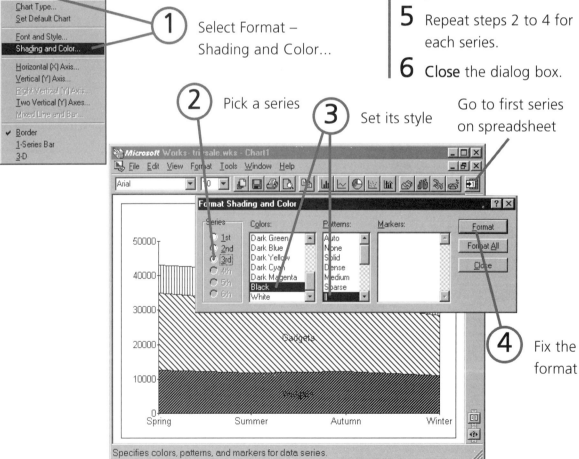

Select Format – Shading and Color...

② Pick a series ③ Set its style

Go to first series on spreadsheet

④ Fix the format

❑ **To change the type**

1 Open the **Format** menu, select **Chart Type** and pick a **Basic Type**.

or

1 Click on a button to choose a type.

2 Open the **Variations** tab.

3 Select the type, checking its appearance in the preview panel.

4 Click [OK].

Tip

If you have a black and white printer, check the effect of your colours and patterns by selecting *Display as Printed* from the *View* menu, or take a Print Preview. What looks good in colour may be awful in black and white.

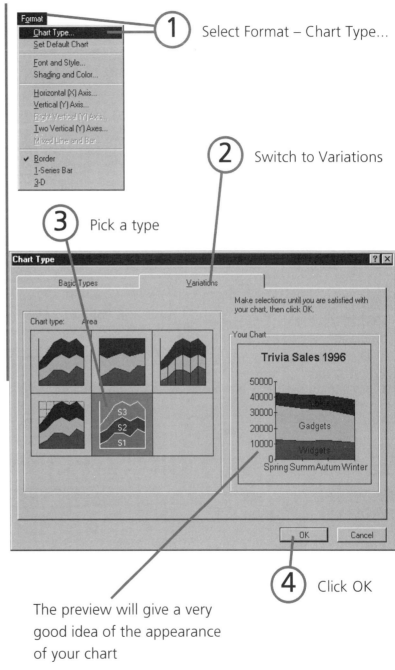

① Select Format – Chart Type...

② Switch to Variations

③ Pick a type

④ Click OK

The preview will give a very good idea of the appearance of your chart

Summary

❑ Data and formulae can be copied either with **Copy** and **Paste** or with **Fill Right** and **Fill Down**.

❑ When formulae are copied, cell and range references are normally adjusted to suit the new positions. If required, references can be absolute, so that they are not changed when the formula is copied.

❑ You can adjust the **height** of rows and the **width** of columns. If reduced to zero, the lines are hidden.

❑ **Hidden** rows and columns can be restored by using **Go To,** to move to a cell in the hidden area, and then increasing the height or width.

❑ Rows, columns and blocks can be **moved** to another position in the sheet. Existing **rows** and **columns** will shuffle up to make room for the moved ones. When **blocks** are moved, they overwrite any existing data.

❑ Rows and columns can be **inserted** or **deleted**.

❑ Blocks of data can be **sorted** on the values held in key columns.

❑ There are a wide variety of **chart types**, designed to meet a range of display needs. They can be selected from the toolbar buttons.

❑ Charts can be given meaningful **Names** to make them easier to find later.

❑ When a chart window is active, the **Format** menu has a new set of commands.

❑ **Colours** and **shading** that work well on screen, do not always work as well when printed. Check your choices by switching to **Display as Printed** view.

7 Working with data

What is a database?

A database is a collection of *records*, each of which will contain data about one person, company, stock item or whatever. The record is split into *fields*, each of which will hold the same kind of data in every record.

The database can be viewed as a *List*, where it will look like a table in a spreadsheet, with each record occupying its own row, and the fields running down the columns. It can also be viewed as a set of *Forms*, where the data for each record is laid out as it might be in a card-index system.

By applying *filters*, you can pull out groups of records that have specified values in particular fields. You could find, for example, all your customers who lived in Macclesfield, or those stock items need to be reordered.

The reports that can be produced from a database may include all items, or a set that have been selected by a filter. They may show all the available data for each record, or only that from selected fields. In this way, the same database can produce mailing labels to send a circular to all your customers, and a list of those who owe money, showing the amounts and the age of each debt.

Data can be copied to and from a spreadsheet, so that you can perform there the calculations that cannot be done in the database. Names, addresses and other data from a database can be combined with standard letters to produced mailshots. (See *Mail Merge*, page 134.)

Tip

There are a number of TaskWizards that will create databases. If you want an address book, accounts or inventory system, check out the TaskWizards before you start to create one from scratch.

Preparing the data

The most important stage in creating a database takes place off-screen. You must have your data organised thoroughly first, before you start to think about form and report designs.

The key questions are:

● What do you want to store?

● What do you want to be able to get out of it?

Data must be broken down into the smallest units that you might want to sort on or search for. If you are storing people's names, for instance, you would normally break them into three fields, Title, Initials (or Forenames) and Surname. The records could then be sorted alphabetically (by Surname), and you could search for someone by their Forename or Surname. It is crucial to get this right from the very start, as you cannot split data up, once it has been typed in.

Works stores database data in the same way that it stores spreadsheet data, and it can display it using the same range of formats. The main ones are:

● Text

● Number

● Date

When you create the database, set a format for each field that will suit its data. Put dates in a text field, and you cannot do much with them. Put them in a Date field, and you can sort records into date order, or search for those before or after a given date .

Creating a database

Plan the structure of your database, and write down the names and formats of the fields it will have. Take a sample of your data and check that it will fit into your structure. Does it work? Yes, then it time to put it into Works.

Start a new Database

Pick a Format   Type a Fieldname

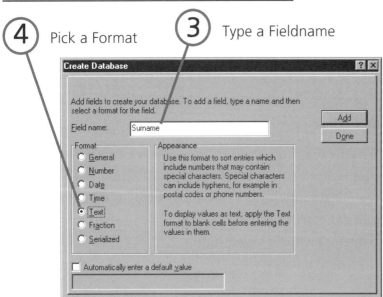

Basic steps

1 Startup Works, or open the **File** menu and select **New**.

2 Go to **Works Tools** and click on **Database**.

3 Type the **Fieldname** for your first field.

4 Set a suitable **Format**.

5 With *Date, Time* and *Number* formats, select an **Appearance**.

6 Click Add

7 Repeat for all fields.

8 Click Done

9 Before you have done too much work on the database, save it.

Take note

Mistakes are not permanent! You can change a field's format in List or Form Design view. Field names can also be changed later.

Tip

If you want to give ID numbers to your records, include a Serialized field. This will automatically number each new record as you create it.

⑤ Set the Appearance

⑥ Click Add

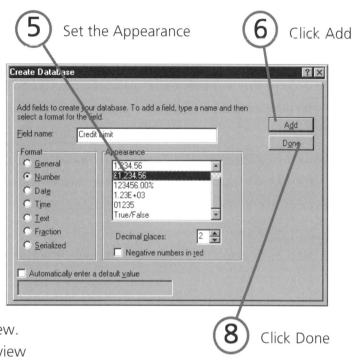

The new database opens in List view. You may want to switch to Form view for easier data entry. (See page 107.)

⑧ Click Done

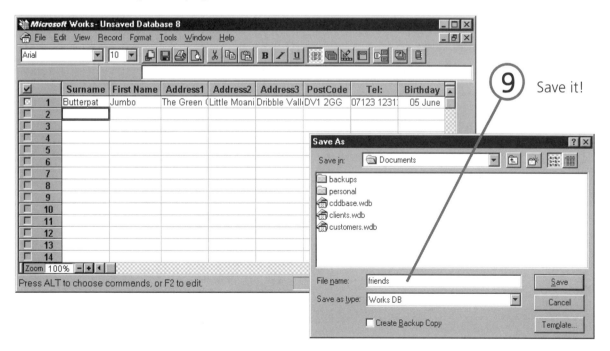

⑨ Save it!

List and Form views

Watch out for:

In List view you can see a screenful of records at a time, though not all of the fields will necessarily be in sight. It is useful when you want to check, or edit, the values in the same fields of different records, and it is simpler to hunt through the database when you can see 15 or 20 records at a time.

The view looks like a spreadsheet, and is handled in much the same way. Things are not exactly the same – the main differences are given on the left.

You can adjust the heights of records and the widths of fields, and note that the changes you make here are not carried over into the form view. You can also move, insert and delete records and fields. All of these operations are carried out as with the rows and columns of the spreadsheet. (See *Adjusting the layout*, page 91.)

There are no Format options on the short menu in List view. Use the Format menu if you want to reformat fields.

❑ **Fonts, borders and shading** cannot be applied to a single cell or block. They always apply to whole fields.

❑ **When sorting,** do not select a block. The sort always works on the whole database.

❑ **Insert Record** 📇 **Delete Record** 📇 and **Insert Field** 📇 have buttons. There is no button for **Delete Field** as they don't want to make this too easy. Use **Record – Delete Field,** or delete it in Form Design view.

Click to go to Form view

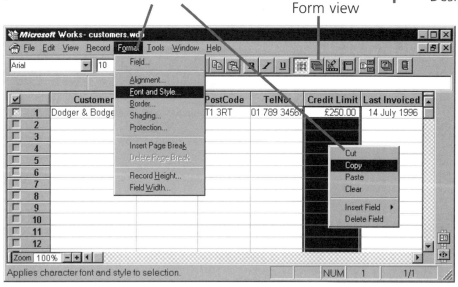

106

Basic steps

Using Form view

- **To edit a field**

1 Move to the record.

2 Move to the field.

3 Either press **[F2]** or click the insertion point into the text in the entry line.

4 When you have done, click ☑ or press **[Enter]** to accept the changes, click ☒ or press **[Escape]** to leave it unchanged.

- **To move with keys**

[Tab] - next field

[Shift]+[Tab] - previous field

[Ctrl]+[PageDown] - next record

[Ctrl]+[PageUp] - previous record

[Ctrl]+[Home] - first record

[Ctrl]+[End] - last record

The Form view is generally the best one to use when entering data or updating records. You would normally be working on one record at a time, and all its details will be to hand. You can easily move between fields and between adjacent records, either with the mouse or the keyboard.

When you want to get a wider view of the database, or make comparisons between records, switch to List view by clicking ▦ on the toolbar.

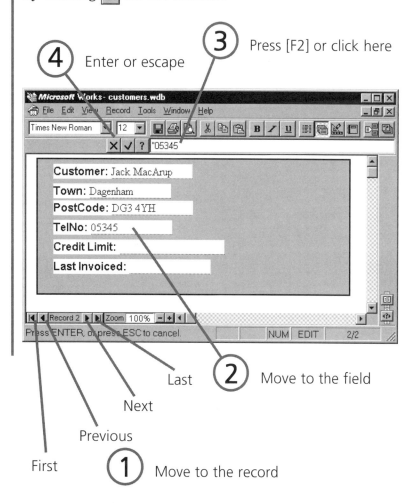

④ Enter or escape
③ Press [F2] or click here
② Move to the field
① Move to the record
Last
Next
Previous
First

Designing the form

When you start a new database, the system sets up a simple form. At any point you can go into Form Design view to change the layout, add *labels* (headings, notes or other text), *graphics* – even new *fields*, if required.

Design the form with screen use in mind. You can print it, but most of your database printing will be as reports, or mailing labels and mailmerge letters via the word processor.

Selecting fields and other items

As elsewhere in Works, you must select items before you can change their format, move and resize them.

❑ **To select a set of adjacent objects**

1 Point to the top left of the enclosing area.

2 Drag to draw an outline around them.

❑ **To select a set of scattered items**

3 Click on the first item.

4 Hold **[Ctrl]** and click on the rest. If you pick one by mistake, click again to deselect it.

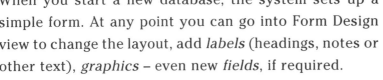

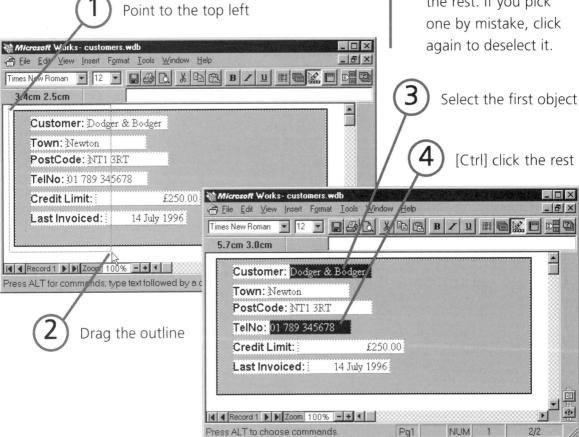

Point to the top left

Drag the outline

Select the first object

[Ctrl] click the rest

Basic steps

❏ To move fields

1 Select the field(s).

2 Move the pointer over the field until the DRAG prompt shows.

3 Hold down the mouse button and move to the new location.

4 Release to drop the field.

❏ To resize a field

1 Select a single field.

2 Move the pointer to an edge to get the RESIZE arrow.

3 Drag the outline to required size.

4 Release the button.

Adjusting the layout

Items can be moved at any time, even after you have started to enter data. Fields can also be resized if you find that data items are larger – or smaller – than anticipated. Changing the width only changes how much is displayed. It has no effect on the data in the fields.

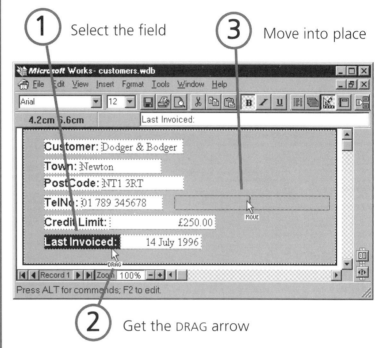

① Select the field   ③ Move into place

② Get the DRAG arrow

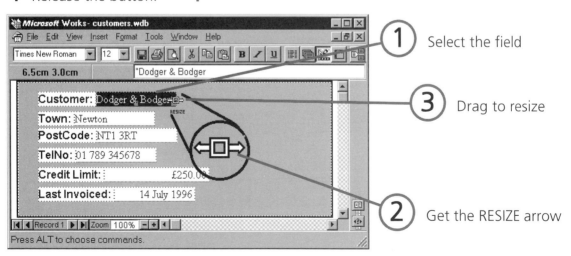

① Select the field

③ Drag to resize

② Get the RESIZE arrow

Presentation

The form can be enhanced in a number of ways:

● **Fonts** and **Alignments** are set here the same as elsewhere – select the items and adjust the settings.

● **Rectangles** can be added to give a background or decorative border around a set of fields.

● **Shading** can be set for fields and the form itself.

● **Borders** can be applied to fields or labels.

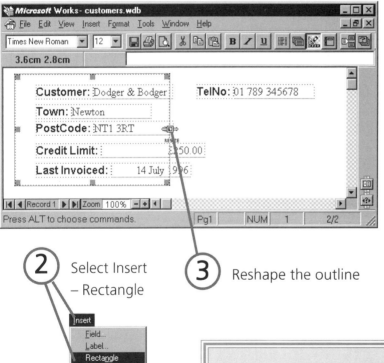

① Get the right part of the form into view

② Select Insert – Rectangle

③ Reshape the outline

Basic steps

❑ **To add a rectangle**

1 Adjust the position of the form in the window so that you can see the place where the rectangle is to go.

2 Open the **Insert** menu and select **Rectangle**.

3 A shadow rectangle will be dropped into the top left corner. Drag it and resize it as required.

4 Right click on the rectangle for its short menu and select **Borders** or **Shading**. Set its line style and background colour.

5 Open the **Format** menu and use **Send to Back** to put the rectangle behind your fields.

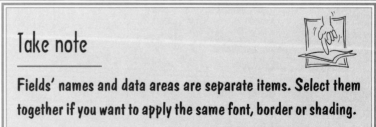

Take note

Fields' names and data areas are separate items. Select them together if you want to apply the same font, border or shading.

110

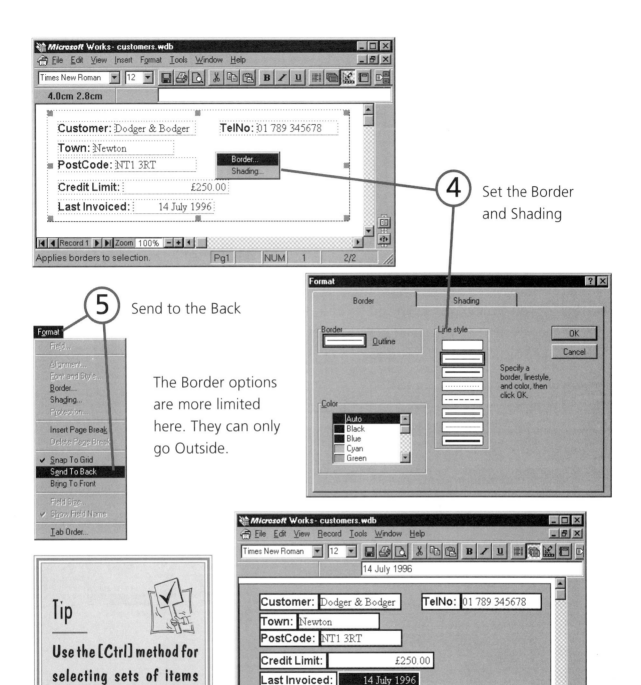

④ Set the Border and Shading

⑤ Send to the Back

The Border options are more limited here. They can only go Outside.

Tip

Use the [Ctrl] method for selecting sets of items inside a rectangle. If you try to drag an outline you tend to select the rectangle itself by mistake.

This rectangle has with light grey solid shading; the data areas have thick borders and are filled with white.

Searching for records

If you want to find a record, or pick out a set of records that share some common values, then you must create a Filter. In this you define what value, or range of values, you are looking for in a particular field. At the simplest you might look for the person with the surname "Jones", or pick out all those customers whose debts were over their credit limits.

For the first of these, you would search the *Customer* field, using the comparison "is equal to" with the value "Jones".

For the second example, you would search the *Amount Owing* field, using the comparison "is greater than" and comparing it to the *Credit Limit* field.

If you want to get more complicated, you might set up a filter to find, for example, those clients in Manchester that do not owe money and haven't received a vist from the rep in the last month.

Filters are saved with the database and can be recalled and reused later, so even if it takes you a little while to set up a filter to pick out exactly the right set of records, at least you only have to do it once.

1 Open the **Tools** menu and select **Filters...** or click 🗗 to open the **Filters** dialog box.

2 Click ⎡ New Filter... ⎤ – you won't need to for your very first filter.

3 Give the filter a name to remind you what sort of records it finds.

4 From the **Field name** list, pick the field that contains the values you are looking for.

5 Pull down the **Comparison** list and pick a comparison.

6 Type a value or a field name into the **Compare To** slot.

7 Click ⎡ Apply Filter ⎤

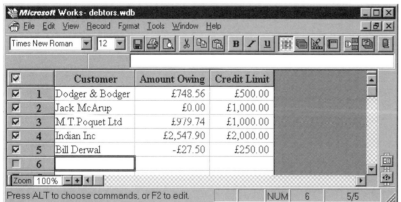

The examples shown here are based on this set of records.

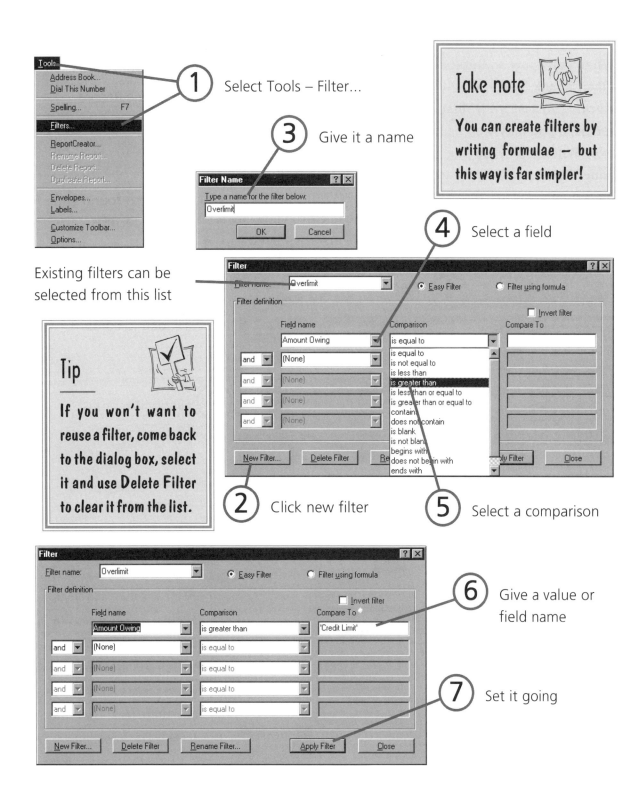

Select Tools – Filter...

Give it a name

Take note

You can create filters by writing formulae – but this way is far simpler!

Select a field

Existing filters can be selected from this list

Tip

If you won't want to reuse a filter, come back to the dialog box, select it and use Delete Filter to clear it from the list.

Click new filter

Select a comparison

Give a value or field name

Set it going

Working with filters

When you apply a filter for the very first time, you may be taken aback by the result – especially if you have been working in List view. Instead of having a screen full of records, you may well be faced with only the odd one or two! Where have all the other 10,000 of your records gone? Don't panic. They are all safe, it's just that the only ones on display are those that match the requirements of the filter. You can bring all the records back into view, or switch so that those that didn't match are displayed – and the matching ones are hidden.

Basic steps

❑ **To restore the full set**

1 Open the **Record** menu.

2 Select **Show** then **All Records**.

❑ **To switch found and hidden records**

1 Open the **Record** menu.

2 Select **Show** then **Hidden Records**.

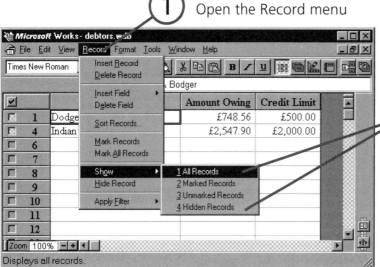

① Open the Record menu

② Show All, or just the hidden ones

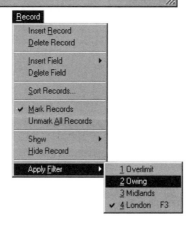

Tip

When you want to reuse a filter, select it from the Record – Apply Filter menu.

Take note

After a Filter has been applied, you only see the records that match the search requirements. If you produce a report now, only these records will be included in the output.

Basic steps

❑ **To mark a record**

1 Click in the box to its left.

❑ **To mark a set**

2 Apply a filter to select the set, then click the top left checkbox.

❑ **To display marked records**

3 Open the **Record** menu, select **Show** then **Marked Records**.

Marking records

Simple filters are good for finding sets of records that match one criterion. If you want to find records that match two or more alternative criteria, there are two approaches.

● Create multi-line filters, linking the lines by OR. E.g., the search might be for "Town is equal to Leeds" OR "Town is equal to London". This can get complicated.

● Create and apply several simple filters, and after each has been run, mark the records that are filtered out. You can then display all marked records, to bring together the results of the separate filters.

Tip

Sometimes it is easier to filter out the records you do not want – rather than those that you do. If you mark them, then Show the Unmarked Records, you will see the ones you wanted.

② Mark all displayed records

① Mark the record

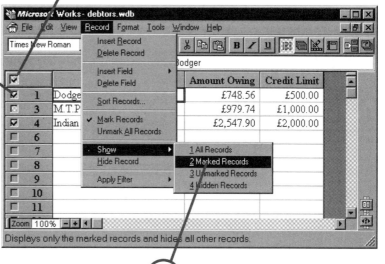

③ Display all marked records

Reporting out

The database's report routines produce lists of the data held in the records. You have a little control over the layout, but full control of the content. You can:

● select the fields to be included in the reports,

● sort and group on one or more fields,

● restrict the report to filtered, or marked, records,

● include a variety of summary statistics.

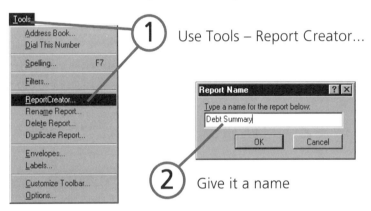

Use Tools – Report Creator...

Give it a name

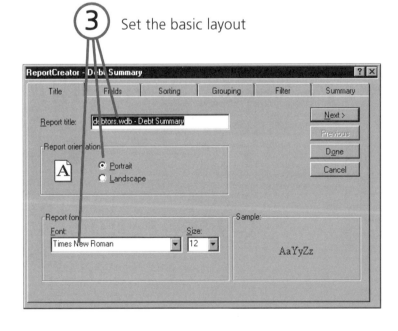

Set the basic layout

Basic steps

1 Open the **Tools** menu and select **Report Creator** ...

2 Type in a name for your report.

❑ Work through the tabs, clicking Next > after each.

3 On the **Title** tab, check and edit the basic layout – title, page orientation and font.

4 On the **Fields** tab, select the field to be included and click Add > after each.

5 On the **Sorting** tab, if you want the output sorted, select a field to **Sort by** and set **Ascending** or **Descending** order.

6 On the **Grouping** tab, if you have set a *Sort by* field, you can also opt to group on this field. Use this where records may have the same value in the *Sort by* field, e.g. Town.

7 On the **Filter** tab, select the set of records to be output. These can be all records, the current displayed set or those from a filter.

8 On the **Summary** tab, select a field for which you want one or more summary figures.

9 Tick the **Summaries** you want for that field.

10 Repeat 8 and 9 for all the fields that are to have summaries.

④ Add fields to the list

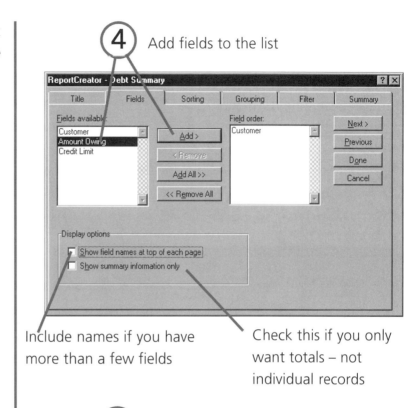

Include names if you have more than a few fields

Check this if you only want totals – not individual records

⑤ Sort the records into an order?

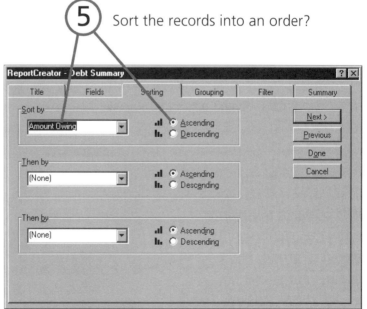

Tip

Use multiple sorts where you have a lot of records – e.g., a club database might be sorted by category of member, sex, then alphabetically by surname.

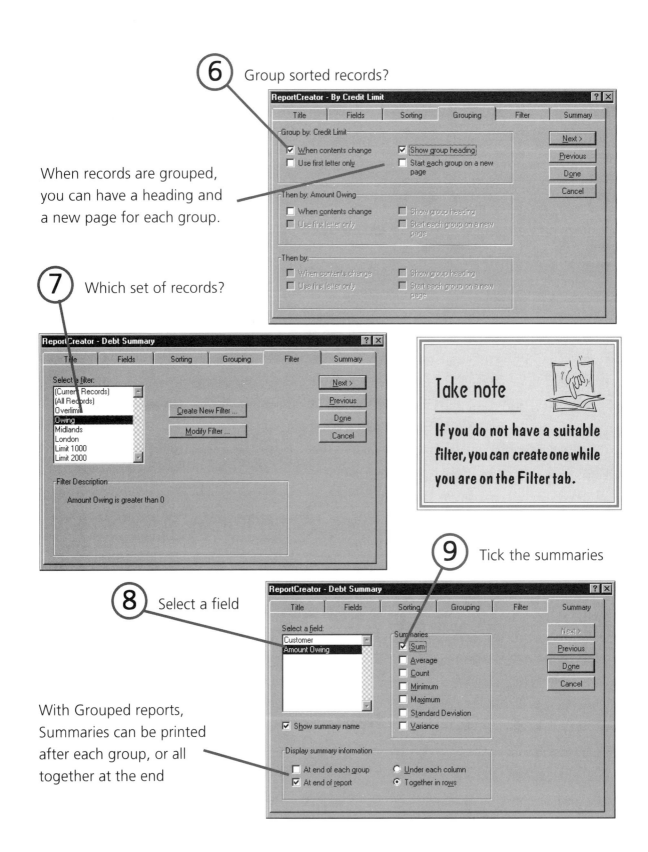

⑥ Group sorted records?

When records are grouped, you can have a heading and a new page for each group.

⑦ Which set of records?

Take note

If you do not have a suitable filter, you can create one while you are on the Filter tab.

⑨ Tick the summaries

⑧ Select a field

With Grouped reports, Summaries can be printed after each group, or all together at the end

118

Improved outputs

When the report is complete, you will be offered a preview – use it. If you do not like the appearance, you can adjust it in Report view. Titles and headings can be changed if necessary, using the normal editing methods. You can also adjust column widths, change text and number formats and add borders and shading.

Needs Currency format

Could be bigger

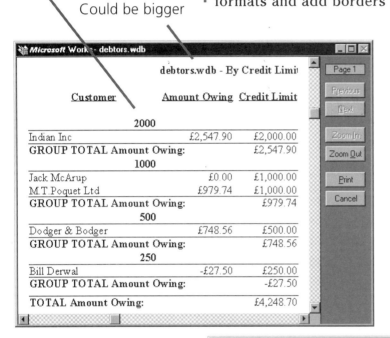

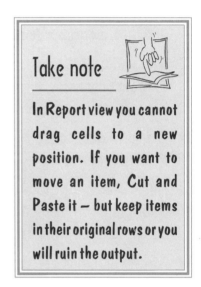

Take note

In Report view you cannot drag cells to a new position. If you want to move an item, Cut and Paste it – but keep items in their original rows or you will ruin the output.

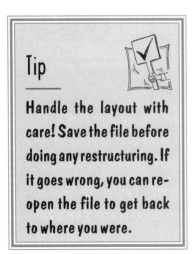

Tip

Handle the layout with care! Save the file before doing any restructuring. If it goes wrong, you can re-open the file to get back to where you were.

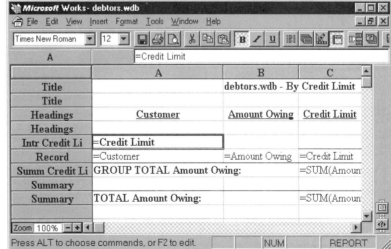

Summary

- ❑ A database is a collection of **records**, with **fields** holding the separate details for each record.

- ❑ If you organise your data before you start to create the database, you will save yourself trouble.

- ❑ You can adjust the appearance of the form through **Form Design** view.

- ❑ Fields' **widths**, and their locations can be adjusted at any time without affecting any data they may hold.

- ❑ Fonts and alignments can be set in the usual way, but borders only apply to individual items. If you want a box around a some items, **Insert** a **Rectangle**.

- ❑ **List view** looks and acts much the same as a spreadsheet.

- ❑ **Filters** search for those records that have particular values in given fields. The comparison can be with actual values, or the values in another field.

- ❑ After a filter has been applied you can only see those records that match. To see the rest again, use **View – Show – All Records**.

- ❑ To reuse a filter , select it from the **Apply Filter** list.

- ❑ **Reports** list the chosen fields for a set of records. They can include summary values.

- ❑ The appearance of the report can be adjusted by editing it in **Report view**.

8 Working together

Inserting objects

Works Charts, tables, Draw, Clip and WordArt graphics, database fields and other objects from other Windows applications can be inserted into word processor documents and database forms. Whatever the type of object, the techniques are much the same. In these pages the objects are bitmap pictures from Paint.

When first inserted, an object will push any existing text out of its way and sit by itself on the left of the page, as above. This is its *In-Line* Wrap mode, and in this you can change its size, drag it to another line and set its Left-Right alignment. The alternative *Absolute* Wrap mode gives you more flexibility. In this mode it can be embedded within text, and positioned anywhere on the page.

(1) Open the Insert menu and select the object type

❑ **To insert an object**

1 Place the insertion pointer where you want the object to go.

2 Open the **Insert** menu and select the type of object.

3 Find or create the object file – techniques vary with the type of object.

❑ **To change Wrap mode**

1 Highlight the object.

2 Open the **Format** menu and select **TextWrap**.

3 Click the **Absolute** icon

4 Set the **Position**.

Take note

Table, Chart, ClipArt and the other options on the Insert menu are all objects. The "Objects..." option handles these plus sound, video and graphics files, and documents produced by other non-Works applications.

Formatting objects

❑ **To set an exact size**

5 Open the **Format** menu and select **Picture**.

6 Bring the **Size** panel to the front and type in the required values for either **Size** or **Scaling**.

Objects can be resized or moved with the usual mouse methods (see *Adjusting the layout*, page 109), but can be adjusted more accurately through the Format options.

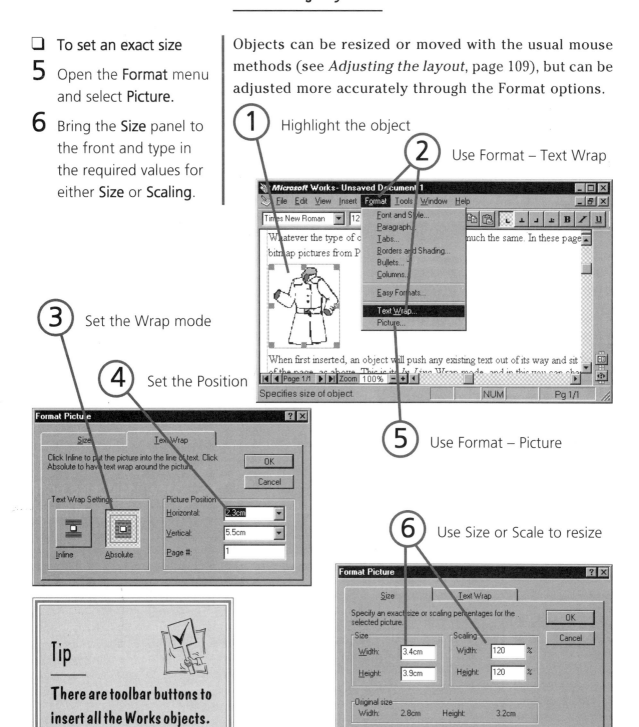

① Highlight the object

② Use Format – Text Wrap

③ Set the Wrap mode

④ Set the Position

⑤ Use Format – Picture

⑥ Use Size or Scale to resize

Tip

There are toolbar buttons to insert all the Works objects.

ClipArt

The ClipArtGallery can handle graphics produced by different packages and stored in different formats, and there are no limitations on size. They are displayed in the Gallery as 'thumbnails', but are restored to their normal size when inserted into a document. The initial set supplied with Works contains around 300 images – there should be something here to meet most situations!

1 Select **Insert – ClipArt** or click 🖼 to open the **ClipArtGallery**.

2 Select a category

3 Scroll through the thumbnails and select an image.

4 Click [Insert]

❏ **Searching for an image**

5 Click [Find...]

6 Type a word that you might expect to be in the **Description**.

7 Click [Find Now]

8 Continue from Step 3

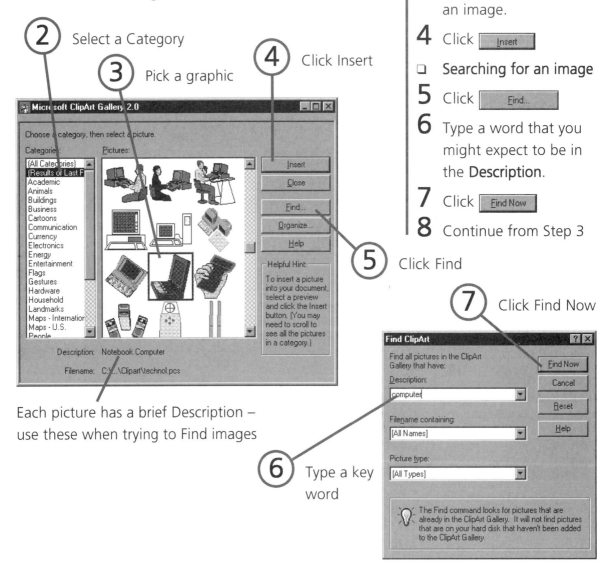

② Select a Category

③ Pick a graphic

④ Click Insert

⑤ Click Find

⑥ Type a key word

⑦ Click Find Now

Each picture has a brief Description – use these when trying to Find images

124

Basic steps

1 In the **Gallery** dialox box, click [Organize...]

❏ **To add all your pictures**

2 Click [Update Pictures...]

3 The update will search your hard drives. Tick the boxes if you want it to check **Network** and **Removable drives**.

4 Click [Update]. Wait!

❏ **To add selectively**

5 Click [Add Pictures...]

6 Browse for the file.

7 At the **Properties** panel, type a **Description**.

8 Set one or more **Categories** for the picture.

9 Click [OK]

Adding pictures

If you have other pictures stored in your computer and want to make them accessible through the Gallery, you can easily add them – either all at once, or selectively.

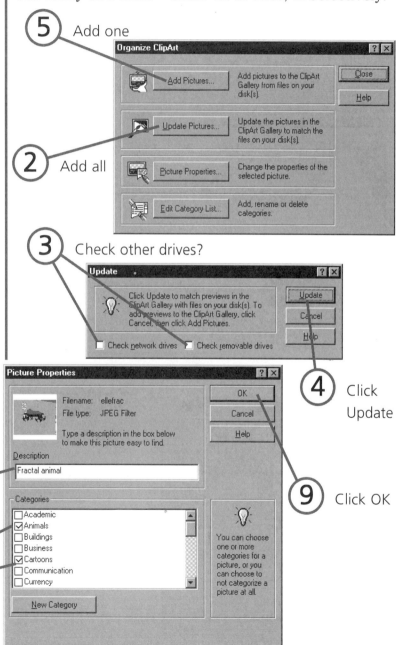

⑤ Add one

④ Click Update

⑨ Click OK

⑦ Describe it

⑧ Set the Categories

MS-Draw

If you are used to Paint, the first thing to realise is that Draw is different. With Paint, anything you add to the picture covers whatever is beneath and becomes a permanent part of the image – just as if you were painting on canvas. In Draw, each object remains separate and can be moved, resized, recoloured or deleted at any time

Basic steps

1 Open the **Insert** menu and select **Drawing** or click

2 Select a tool to create an object.

3 Adjust its size, position colours and font as necessary.

4 Repeat steps 2 and 3 to create your image.

5 Use **File – Update** to copy the picture into your document.

6 Open the **File** menu and select **Exit and Return to...**

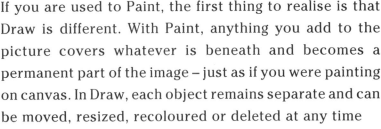

① Select Insert – Drawing

② Pick a tool

Select existing objects

Zoom in

Line

Closed shapes

Polygon

Text

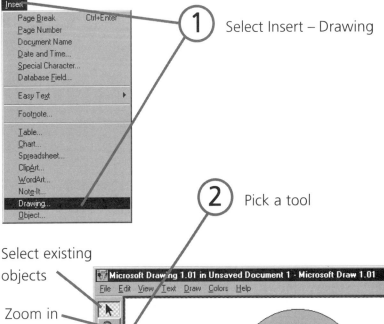

Hold a corner block to resize. Drag anywhere on the object to move it.

Current colours

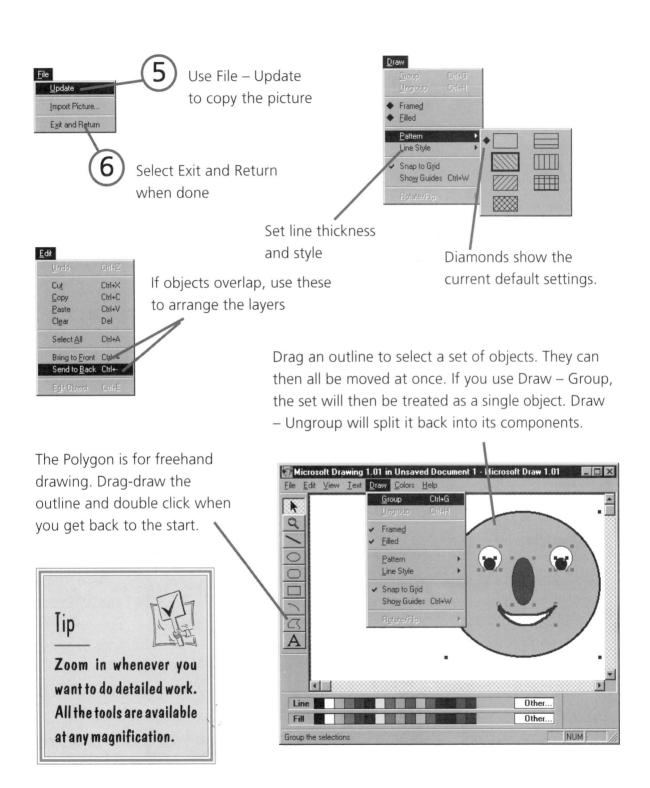

5 Use File – Update to copy the picture

File
Update
Import Picture...
Exit and Return

6 Select Exit and Return when done

Draw
Group   Ctrl+G
Ungroup   Ctrl+H
◆ Framed
◆ Filled
Pattern   ▶
Line Style   ▶ ◆
Snap to Grid
Show Guides Ctrl+W
Rotate/Flip

Set line thickness and style

Diamonds show the current default settings.

Edit
Undo   Ctrl+Z
Cut   Ctrl+X
Copy   Ctrl+C
Paste   Ctrl+V
Clear   Del
Select All   Ctrl+A
Bring to Front Ctrl+=
Send to Back   Ctrl+-
Edit Object   Ctrl+E

If objects overlap, use these to arrange the layers

Drag an outline to select a set of objects. They can then all be moved at once. If you use Draw – Group, the set will then be treated as a single object. Draw – Ungroup will split it back into its components.

The Polygon is for freehand drawing. Drag-draw the outline and double click when you get back to the start.

Tip

Zoom in whenever you want to do detailed work. All the tools are available at any magnification.

Microsoft Drawing 1.01 in Unsaved Document 1 - Microsoft Draw 1.01

File Edit View Text Draw Colors Help

Group   Ctrl+G
Ungroup   Ctrl+H
✓ Framed
✓ Filled
Pattern   ▶
Line Style   ▶
✓ Snap to Grid
Show Guides Ctrl+W
Rotate/Flip   ▶

Line   Other...
Fill   Other...

Group the selections   NUM

WordArt

With WordArt, text can be rotated, distorted, shadowed and patterned. The process is fiddly, but it does allow you to make a real splash with text. You could put it to good use it for invitations, adverts, posters, newsletters and the like.

The system has a couple of flaws:

● you cannot resize of the object from within WordArt, and a different effect may require a different size;

● the proportions of the object stay constant, even though the text may occupy only a small part of it if it has been rotated or curved

Basic steps

1 Open the **Insert** menu and select **WordArt** or click 🖅

2 Type your text into the WordArt window

3 Click ⟨ Update Display ⟩ to write it to the page.

4 Point and click back into your document.

5 Select the WordArt object and resize it.

6 Double click on the object to return to WordArt to set the effects. (Expect to do steps 5 and 6 several times before you have finished!)

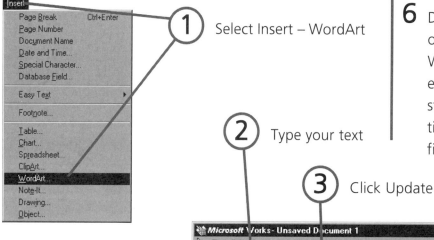

① Select Insert – WordArt

② Type your text

③ Click Update

Displays a set of symbols and other special characters

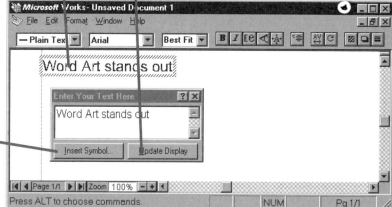

The buttons

Ee   Makes lower case letters the same height as capitals.

◁   Rotates the text through 90 degrees.

·A·   Makes the text expand to fill the shape.

AV   Sets the tracking – the spacing between characters.

C   Sets rotation and arc angles through the Special Effects panel. (See right.)

▨   Sets the fill patterns for the letters.

▣   Sets the shadow style (See right.)

≡   Sets the style of the outline of the letters.

This has been curved, with the arc flattened to 30°, then given a fill pattern, thin outline and simple black shadow.

Text effects

These can all be set from the toolbar – either from the buttons or the three drop-down lists. The font and size lists as are normal, except that there is a **Best Fit** size – generally the best option. The leftmost list is new.

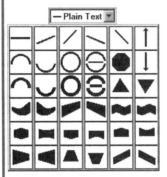

This sets the overall shape made by the text. The shape may well be much smaller than the object's outline – be prepared to enlarge it.

With curved text, a smaller Arc Angle flattens the curve.

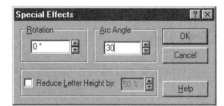

The on-the-ground shadows do not work well with shaped text. Keep these for straight text.

Note-It

This adds an icon, with a note attached. Double-clicking on the icon makes the note pop up in the top left of the screen.Use them for pinning comments onto a document that is being passed (electronically) around the office.

Notes can be moved, resized and deleted, just like any other object. You can also edit their text and icon.

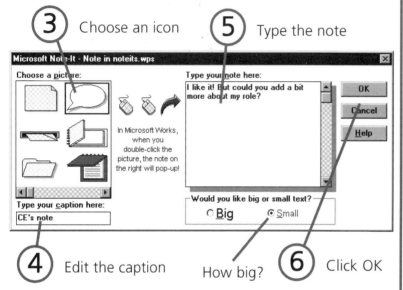

③ Choose an icon ⑤ Type the note

④ Edit the caption   How big?   ⑥ Click OK

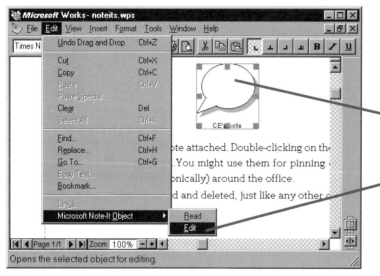

❑ **To add a note**

1 Place the insertion point where you want to add the note.

2 Open the **Insert** menu and select **Note-It** or click 🖼

3 Select an **icon**.

4 Change the **caption** – if you do not want one, erase the prompt.

5 Type your **note**.

6 Click ▢ OK ▢.

❑ **To edit a note**

7 Select the note's icon.

8 Open the **Edit** menu and select **Microsoft Note-It Object**, then **Edit**. This takes you back into the Note-It dialog box.

⑦ Select theNote-It

⑧ Use Edit – Note-It Object – Edit

130

Basic steps

1 Open the **Insert** menu and select **Object...**

Either

2 Select **Create from file**, and browse through you system for the one you want.

3 Check **Link** if you want the object to be updated when the original file changes.

Or

4 Select **Create new**, and pick the application.

5 When the object is created, click back into your Works document, or use **Update** and **Exit** options (names vary) on the application's **File** menu.

The list should display all the suitable applications on your system.

Linked objects

A *linked* object is one that was created by another application, and that retains its connection to that application within its Works document. Double-clicking on the object activates the link and opens the original application so that the object can be edited.

Linking can be extended beyond the Microsoft add-ons to any other software that can handle the Windows link mechanism – and most new Windows applications can.

When you insert an object, you will be offered the choice of creating a new one or using an existing file. If you create from file, you will be given the option to link.

2 Browse for the file   **3** Link it?

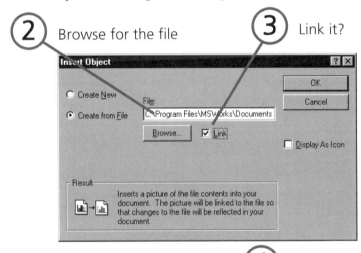

4 Pick the application

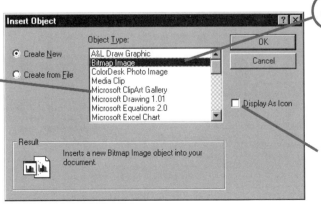

Use *icon* displays where you want to link to a file, but do not display it in your document.

Spreadsheets

The formatting facilities in the spreadsheet are not bad, but if you want a really good-looking report from a spreadsheet, the simplest solution is to write its text in the word processor and insert ranges and charts from the sheet. To be able to do this, the ranges that form the tables of data must have been given names within the spreadsheet. The charts may still be called Chart1, Chart2 and so on, though meaningful names for these will also make them easier to find when you are inserting.

Basic steps

❑ **To insert a range**

1 Open the spreadsheet.

2 Return to the word processor document by clicking on it or by picking its name from the **Window** menu.

3 Open the **Insert** menu and select **Spreadsheet** or **Chart...**

4 Set the **Use an existing...** option

5 Select the spreadsheet from the left hand list.

6 Select the range or the chart from the list on the right.

7 Click ☐ OK ☐.

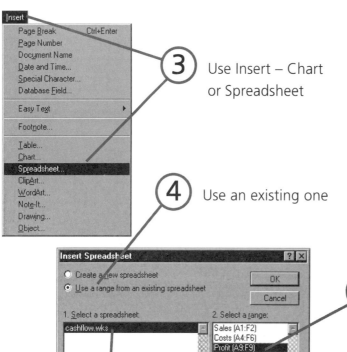

③ Use Insert – Chart or Spreadsheet

④ Use an existing one

⑤ Select the spreadsheet

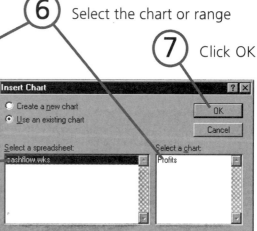

⑥ Select the chart or range

⑦ Click OK

Basic steps

1 Open the Insert menu and select Chart... or click

2 Select Create a new

3 Click [OK]

   You will be told that data is needed.

4 Enter the headings and data for the table.

5 Select the data

6 Click the Chart icon at the bottom left.

7 You will be presented with the standard New Chart dialog box. Set the options as in the spreadsheet.

8 Click into the document to resize and position the chart.

If you are working in the word processor and have a small set of data that you want to present as a chart, the simplest solution is to use Insert Chart. This gives you enough spreadsheet facilities to do the job.

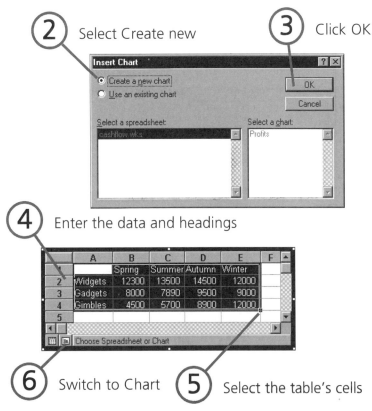

② Select Create new

③ Click OK

④ Enter the data and headings

	A	B	C	D	E	F
		Spring	Summer	Autumn	Winter	
2	Widgets	12300	13500	14500	12000	
3	Gadgets	8000	7890	9500	9000	
4	Gimbles	4500	5700	8900	12000	
5						

Choose Spreadsheet or Chart

⑥ Switch to Chart   ⑤ Select the table's cells

Take note

If you want a formatted table of data in a document, use Insert – Table. All the normal spreadsheet tools and menus are available when editing the table.

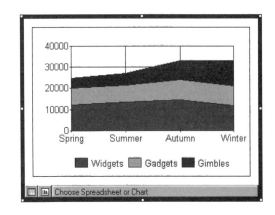

Mail merge

With Mail merge, you take information from a database and slot it into a standard layout to produce mailing labels or personalised letters. With Works, a mail merge is simple to organise. The difficult part is composing a letter that people do not throw straight into the bin.

(3) Stop when you want some data

(4) Select Insert – Database Field...

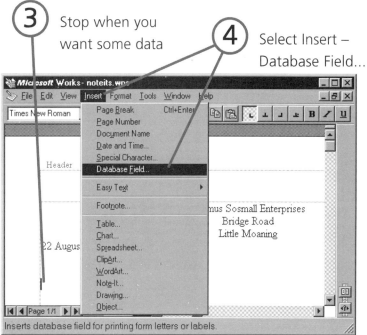

(5) Select and Insert each field

(7) Return to editing

If the database is not shown here...

... click this button to go and find it.

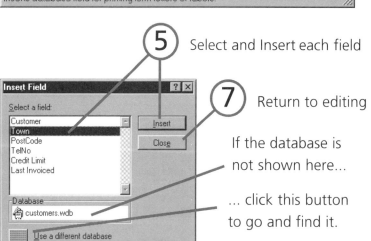

1 Open the database. Filter or mark to select the records you want.

2 Start up a new document for your label or form letter

3 Write your text, stopping when you get to where you want to pull in data.

4 Open the **Insert** menu and select **Database Field..**

5 Select a field and click ☐ Insert ☐

6 If you want other fields straight after the first, insert them.

7 Click ☐ Close ☐ to return to the text.

8 Repeat steps 3 to 7 as needed.

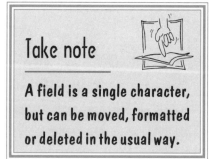

Take note

A field is a single character, but can be moved, formatted or deleted in the usual way.

134

Basic steps

Printing

1 Open the **Tools** menu and select **Form Letter...**

2 Go to the **Recipients** tab

3 Select the set to be merged.

4 Go to the **Printing** tab to preview and print

Before you print your letters, select your recipients. These can be all the people in the database, those currently displayed or marked, or those selected by a filter.

You should also preview the letter to check that you have inserted the right fields in the right places!

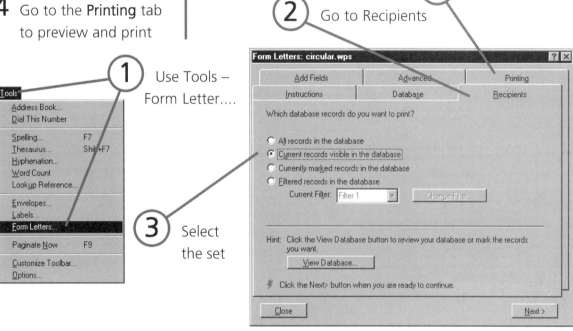

④ Go to Printing

② Go to Recipients

① Use Tools – Form Letter....

③ Select the set

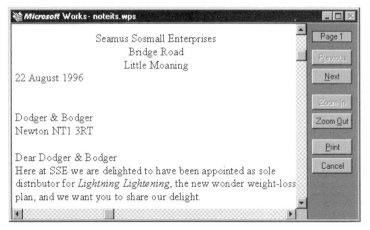

You can also insert fields and get help on mail merge from this dialog box.

A Preview of the mail merge letter, showing the first customer's details, pulled in from the database.

Summary

❑ Objects can be **inserted** into word processor documents and database forms. Double-clicking on them or using the **Edit – Object** command will reopen the application that created them.

❑ Objects can be resized and repositioned. They can sit in lines free of text or have text wrapped round them.

❑ The **ClipArt Gallery** has hundreds of ready-made images to choose from. It can also handle any others you have on your system.

❑ **Draw** is an object-base graphics package. With it you can build up pictures out of lines, circles, rectangles and closed polygons.

❑ **WordArt** can produce text that is curved, shaped, stretched, shadowed and patterned.

❑ **Note-It** lets you place icons, with pop-up notes, on your word-processed documents.

❑ Objects produced by other Windows applications can be **linked** into your files.

❑ You can insert **Charts** and **Ranges** from an open spreadsheet. The display in the document will be updated if the spreadsheet is edited.

❑ You can create new **Charts** or **Tables** within the word-processor, but using the normal spreadsheet facilities.

❑ By inserting **Database Fields** into a form letter, you can create mail merge documents.

9 Working on-line

Setting up

Working on-line is getting easier, though you will still meet more jargon here than in any other application. Works does its best to simplify the process and you can ignore much of the jargon. If you have the phone number and the basic communications settings of the service that you want to access, then you should be able to get on-line – the terminal settings may need tweaking to get the best display, but at least you should get through.

Basic steps

- ❏ **To start a new file**
1. Type the **Phone number**, including spaces and dashes (-) if you like.
2. Type a **Name** for your reference.
3. Click OK .
4. The system will try to connect you. This first time, click Cancel and check the settings before going on-line.

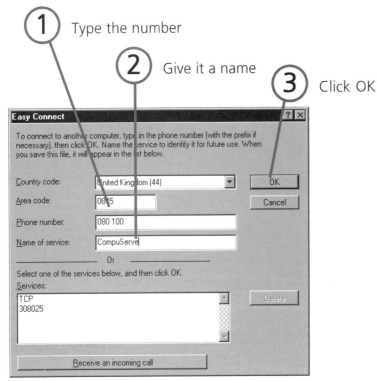

① Type the number

② Give it a name

③ Click OK

④ Cancel, unless you are sure the settings are right

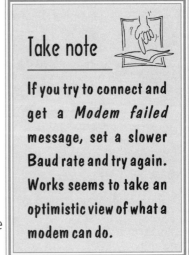

Take note

If you try to connect and get a *Modem failed* message, set a slower Baud rate and try again. Works seems to take an optimistic view of what a modem can do.

Communication settings

Basic steps

1 Click [icon] or open the **Settings** menu and select **Communication**

2 Click [Properties...].

3 On the **General** tab, reduce the **Baud rate**, if you are having difficulty getting on-line.

4 On the Connection tab, set the **Data** and **Parity Bits** as specified by the comms service.

Communication settings

You will normally only have to adjust two settings:

Baud rate – the speed at which data travels. If you cannot connect at the current rate, try the next lower setting.

Data and **Parity Bits** – There are two common combinations: 7 Data bits, Even Parity, 1 Stop bit; 8 Data bits, No Parity, 1 Stop bit

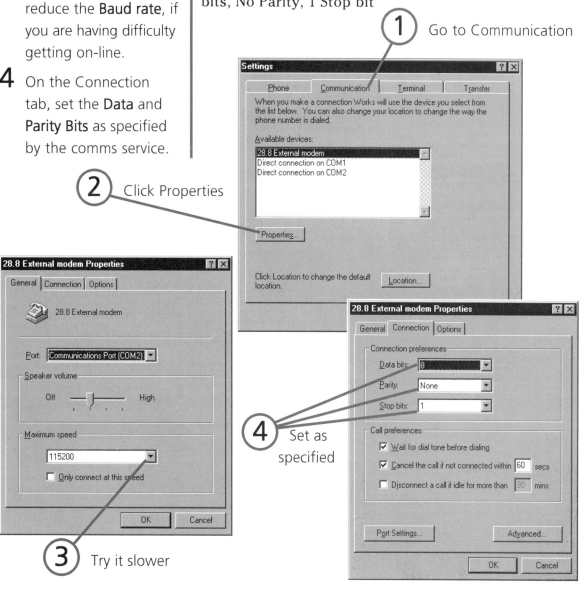

① Go to Communication

② Click Properties

③ Try it slower

④ Set as specified

139

Transfer settings

The Transfer protocol controls the connection between your computer and the one at the other end of the line while a file is being transferred. Both must use the same protocol. XModem is probably the most common, though ZModem – which is more efficient – is increasingly used. Set Zmodem as the default, unless your comms service recommends another.

The one part of this panel that does need your attention is the **Directory**. Set it no so that you do not waste time changing the directory while you are capturing or sending text on-line.

Basic steps

1 Switch to the **Transfer** panel or click 📇 on the toolbar

2 Set the **Protocol** if one is specified by the comms service.

3 Click [Directory...]

4 Choose the directory in which your comms files will be stored.

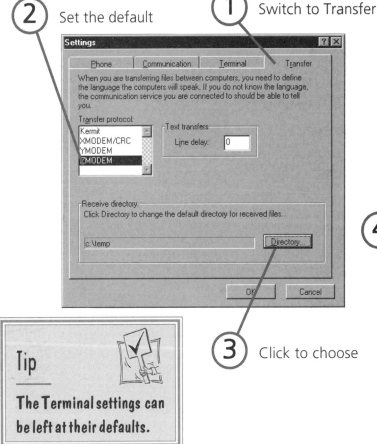

(2) Set the default

(1) Switch to Transfer

(3) Click to choose

Take note

Once you have adjusted the settings, you can connect using *Phone – Dial* or by clicking 🐾

(4) Set the Directory

140

Capturing text

Basic steps

1 Open the **Tools** menu and select **Capture Text...** or click 📷

2 Set the folder if necessary.

3 Type in a **Filename**.

4 Click [Save].

5 Set the incoming text flowing.

6 When you reach the end, open the **Tools** menu and select **End Capture Text**.

The key to successful working on-line is to do as much as possible *off*-line. All the time that you are on-line, you are clocking up phone charges, and perhaps service charges as well. You cannot read the text at the same speed that it comes in – unless you are a very quick reader and have a very slow modem – and you certainly cannot type as fast as it can be sent!

Any time that you have a chunk of text coming down the line, that doesn't require an immediate reply, capture it into a file and deal with it later.

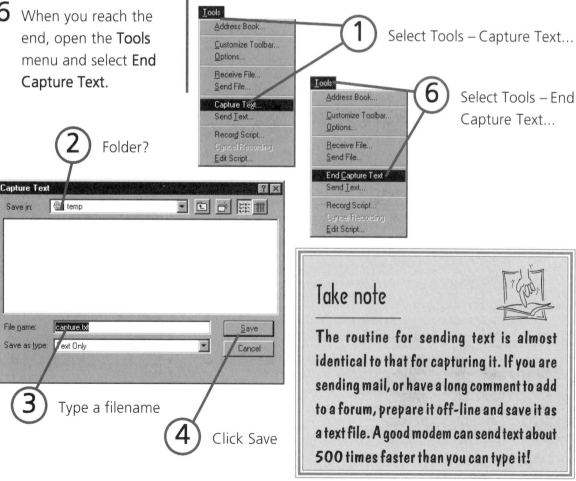

(1) Select Tools – Capture Text...

(6) Select Tools – End Capture Text...

(2) Folder?

(3) Type a filename

(4) Click Save

Take note

The routine for sending text is almost identical to that for capturing it. If you are sending mail, or have a long comment to add to a forum, prepare it off-line and save it as a text file. A good modem can send text about 500 times faster than you can type it!

Transferring binary files

In communications, files fall into two distinct groups – plain text and binaries, which includes graphics, programs, formatted text and everything else. When text is sent, the system only uses 7 bits out of every byte for the data – enough to define the character – and the eight bit can be used for checking purposes. With binary files, all 8 bits are essential. So, when you want to send of receive anything other than a simple text file, you must use one of the binary routines.

❑ **To send a binary file**

1 Make sure that the remote computer is ready to receive your file, and that you are using a compatible transfer protocol.

2 Open the **Tools** menu and select **Send File...** or click ⬚

3 Switch to the right folder if necessary.

4 Select your **file**.

5 Click [Send].

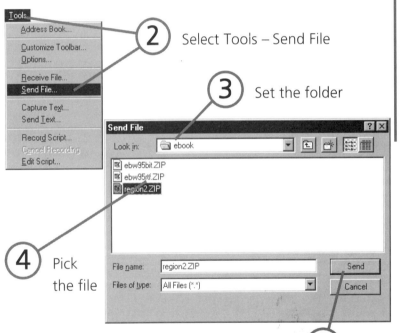

Select Tools – Send File

Set the folder

Pick the file

Click Send

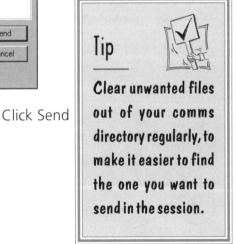

Tip

Clear unwanted files out of your comms directory regularly, to make it easier to find the one you want to send in the session.

Take note

When downloading binary files, use the Receive File routine to set up your system then tell the remote computer to start the transfer.

Basic steps

1 Sign off to close your on-line connection.

2 Open the **Phone** menu and select **Hang Up** or click .

Signing off

When you sign off from your comms service, it closes the connection to them, but does not put the phone back on the hook. Don't forget to hang up! Likewise, don't hang up without first signing off, or you could be running up connection charges even though you are not there.

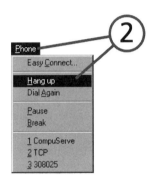

2 Select Phone – Hang Up

Take note

To find out more about on-line communications, why not try one or more of these other Made Simple books:

The Internet for Windows 95 – P.K.McBride, ISBN 0750628359

Internet Resources Made Simple – P.K.McBride, ISBN 0750628367

Designing Internet Home Pages Made Simple – L, Hobbs, ISBN 07506 2941 X

Available from your bookstore now, or direct from the publishers, using your credit card, on 01865 314627.

Summary

❏ Apart from the **Data** and **Parity Bits** and **Baud rate**, most of the default settings should not need changing.

❏ File transfer can controlled by several different protocols. **ZModem** and **XModem** are the two most commonly used.

❏ For the most efficient use of phone time, you should handle as much text as possible *off-line*.

❏ Use **Capture Text** to store incoming text in a file.

❏ Use **Send Text** for any lengthy pieces of text – in fact for anything much more than responses to interactive prompts.

❏ **Binary files** are treated differently from text files. Use the Send and Receive File routines to transfer these.

❏ Don't forget to sign off and **hang up** at the end of a session.

Index